"I love MKs. They are some of the most incre[...]
I had two amazing MKs grow up in our home. [...]
a broad worldview, international travel and li[...] ...language and
culture skills, they often feel that they don't belong—no matter where they are.
They don't entirely fit into the culture where their parents serve—even though
they grew up there—and they feel like foreigners when they go on furlough to their
parents' home country. Many feel most at home on a plane between two countries.
Jeanne Harrison has done a wonderful service to MKs and to the church in this
book, helping us all to understand life from her MK perspective. MKs, missionary
parents, and churches will be blessed by the lessons they learn from Jeanne."

—M. David Sills, DMiss., PhD, AP and Faye Stone Chair of Christian Missions
and Cultural Anthropology, The Southern Baptist Theological Seminary,
and president, Reaching & Teaching International Ministries

"The pain and challenges in the adjustments of missionary kids are real. Jeanne
Harrison has been there and communicates with a sensitivity and relevance that
will speak to current MKs as well as to adult former MKs who are still suffering
from their experiences. A journey of discipleship, *Hiding in the Hallway* challenges
readers to face basic spiritual realities and restores confidence and joy."

—Jerry Rankin, president emeritus, International
Mission Board, Southern Baptist Convention

"Jeanne Harrison addresses the core challenges of the MK lifestyle in a way that
is refreshingly blunt and exceedingly gospel focused. Having worked with MKs
myself for more than 20 years, I believe that when MKs truly understand the
gospel for themselves, they are free to live out all the benefits of their lifestyle.
Hiding in the Hallway challenges the reader to look at their MK experience through
the framework of a God who understands the many unique challenges of the
missionary journey. I personally can't wait to share this book with the hundreds of
MKs and missionary parents in my sphere of ministry."

—Donna Kushner, director of MK2MK, a ministry of Cru

HIDING IN THE HALLWAY

ANCHORING YOURSELF AS AN MK

JEANNE HARRISON

NEW HOPE® PUBLISHERS
Gospel-Centered. Missions-Driven.

BIRMINGHAM, ALABAMA

New Hope® Publishers
PO Box 12065
Birmingham, AL 35202-2065
NewHopePublishers.com
New Hope Publishers is a division of WMU®.

New Hope Publishers serves its authors as they express their views, which may not express the views of the publisher.

Many of the names in the book have been changed to protect the privacy of those individuals. The author has recalled events and conversations that occurred over the course of her life and, although they are relayed as accurately as the author can recall them, are not intended to represent word-for-word transcripts. They are intended to convey the essence of an occurrence.

Library of Congress Cataloging-in-Publication Data

Names: Harrison, Jeannette, 1984- author.
Title: Hiding in the hallway : anchoring yourself as an MK / Jeanne Harrison.
Description: First [edition]. | Birmingham : New Hope Publishers, 2017.
Identifiers: LCCN 2017021503 | ISBN 9781625915313 (permabind)
Subjects: LCSH: Children of missionaries. | Harrison, Jeannette, 1984-
Classification: LCC BV2094.5 .H365 2017 | DDC 266—dc23
LC record available at https://lccn.loc.gov/2017021503

Cover image: Maria Savenko/Shutterstock.com

ISBN-13: 978-1-62591-531-3

N184105 • 0917 • 2M1

To my parents,
Howie and Nance Kauffman,
who gave me roots ... and wings.

TABLE OF CONTENTS

ACKNOWLEDGMENTS

I am indebted to the entire team at New Hope Publishers for taking a chance on a new author; my heartfelt thanks for your availability, tireless efforts, love for Christ, and commitment to excellence. I also want to thank my family at Northway Church for championing me as a writer. This book was written on the backbone of your prayers.

Thank you, Donna Kushner, for your genuine interest in this project in the initial stages, and George Siler, for pointing me in the right direction so this book could see the light of day. Also, thanks, Stephen and Rhoda Keefer, for connecting me with missionary leaders, and Paula Marsteller, for always having a word of encouragement. To David Platt, thank you for writing a *Radical* book that rattled my comfortable life and inspired me to start this work in the first place.

To my parents, Howie and Nance Kauffman, thank you for your constant love, honest counsel, and endless editing—but mostly for moving across the globe more than 40 years ago to faithfully serve Jesus. Your lives taught me how to live mine. Thanks also to my in-laws, Randy and Evelyn Harrison, for cheering me on and graciously babysitting so I could meet deadlines, and to all of my wonderful siblings for your invaluable input and support.

Most of all, thank you to my best friend and all-time favorite man alive, Clint Harrison, for listening (and listening and listening!) to me talk about this book, for believing in me right from the start, for loving me at my finest and my worst, for getting so stinkin' excited about my writing, and for covering me in prayer. I admire you more every single day. And to our beautiful daughters Aubrey, Heidi, Lila, and Reese, without whom my world would be inexpressibly duller. You are the sunshine in my days, the pride of my life, and the delight of my heart!

Finally, to all the MKs whose stories wove together to create this book, thank you. Thank you for sharing your lives with me, for being part of my journey, and for being used by God to impact generations.

MK: missionary kid

Someone raised in a third culture due to parents' missionary work

FOREWORD

Andrea Buczynski
Vice President, Global Leadership Development/HR
Campus Crusade for Christ/Cru

Missionary kids.

Whether you are one or know one (or more!), that description alone tells you something—these are kids who are defined by their parents' vocation. All parents are often judged for their children's behavior. But we don't go around saying, "Hey, he's an engineer kid," or, "She's a real estate kid." Outside of ministry, parenthood is separated from vocation. Missionary kids, like pastors' kids, can end up carrying a burden of expectation—proof positive (or negative) of their parents' qualification as gospel ministers.

Jeanne Harrison knows these pressures intimately. She has lived them. Fifteen years with her parents in the Philippines ended with the shock of returning to the United States. Her candid stories give an inside look from a kid's perspective about the impact of missionary parents' choices on children.

I've seen the struggles Jeanne describes firsthand as families return to the US from overseas assignments. I'm sure you have too. Maybe you've lived through them. Maybe you're living with them now. Kids raised in other countries struggle with reentry. High school or middle school is all about fitting in, being one of the gang. MKs are missing key ingredients toward that—their histories are distinctly different from and unrelated to their peers. Shaped by cultures with different values, these kids often face various struggles. Overwhelmed and insecure, they can get lost in the midst of parents fulfilling their calling.

In every chapter of this book, you will experience Jeanne's heart to change that reality. She effectively calls the adults in their lives to pay attention to missionary kids, not at the expense of fulfilling calling, but to come alongside them with compassion. For us at Cru, this means paying greater attention to families, especially the kids, in light of increasing numbers of families going to and returning from the mission field. Successful sending and reentry is a family process and is not limited to the missionaries themselves. Jeanne brilliantly shows why and points the way to the how.

Both missionary kids and missionary parents have a lot to gain from Jeanne's warm, personal storytelling and teaching, as well as her thoughtful reflection questions. Your experiences may be different! She knows that. In writing this book, Jeanne shines the spotlight on the feelings and experiences of missionary kids who may be "hiding in the hallway," just hoping that someone sees them.

INTRODUCTION

I loved being an MK until the day it cost me something. At the time I would've told you it cost me everything.

I was a teenager being forcibly dragged across the globe so my parents could serve in a new location when I decided I hated airports. I hated airplanes, passports, and all the "buckle-your-seatbelt" instructions I could repeat in my sleep. I hated knowing strangers were going to squeeze my cheeks and tell me how much I'd grown, when on the inside I felt like I was shrinking, disappearing into an ocean of sadness. I hated the terror that churned in my stomach every time I thought about going to a new school and the ache in my chest when I imagined my friends moving on without me.

If I were really honest, I would have admitted I hated missions. I didn't hate the "fun" part—the part where I got to visit exotic places and meet people from different countries. But I hated the confusing part—the part where I felt powerless and misunderstood, drifting between worlds I could never fully claim as my own.

When God first inspired me to write this book, all those feelings bubbled back to the surface. I found myself wondering, "How can I be 32 years old and still be so affected by my upbringing as an MK?" "Why is the MK journey so complicated, and how do we navigate it biblically?"

Immediately God brought one thing to mind: the gospel. It's taken me years to connect the dots between the gospel and my journey as an MK, but I believe the gospel alone is our answer. With this book I want to show you how the gospel speaks to a multitude of MK subjects— from furloughs and farewells to dating, doubt, rootlessness, missional opportunities, and more.

MK, my prayer is that throughout these pages you would encounter Christ in the midst of your unique story. Believe me when I say, I know what it's like to belong everywhere and nowhere. To visit new schools and youth groups where you sit all by yourself. I know what it's like to value places more than things and memories more than realities. But after a journey 30 years in the making, I also know what it's like to be caught up in the splendor of a greater Story. To finally understand my identity and my life in light of Christ's identity and Christ's life. That's what I want for you too. May this book—written with prayers, tears, and gallons of coffee—be an agent of truth and grace in your beautiful life!

CHAPTER 1

WHY I DO (AND DON'T) UNDERSTAND YOU

"Shhh! They'll hear you!" My brother, sister, and I crouched in the hallway of our modest Filipino home. Tall wooden panels separated us from the crowd in the living room, but we had long since discovered that if we pressed our faces between them, we could see everything.

"This is so boring," my brother complained. "What are they even talking about?"

"Who cares?" I whispered, peering at my dad from between the panels. As usual, he was at the front of the room, talking loudly and gesturing with his hands. My mom sat on the sofa, while Filipino men and women filled the rest of the room.

"They're praying!" My sister exclaimed, jabbing me in the ribs. "Hurry up! It's your turn!"

"*Ow!* But I went last time!"

"Just *go!*"

"Oh fine!" I darted out of the hallway, racing on tiptoes toward my mom. I could tell my dad's prayer was nearly over. "Mom!" I hissed. "I know you said not to bother you, but we finished all our dinner, and can we have some ice cream?" Over the years it had been statistically proven that if you asked for ice cream during a meeting the answer was almost guaranteed to be "yes!"

HIDING IN THE HALLWAY

Growing up as an MK in the Philippines, I spent a lot of time on my knees in that hallway. Sometimes I was waiting on my parents, and other times I was just being a nosy kid. I overheard conversations I wasn't supposed to hear and learned lessons nobody meant to teach me. I learned that even adults have problems that make them cry and that my parents were more than just my parents. I learned that they were teachers, counselors, friends, and mentors. I learned that in this great big world of Ministry, everybody had a place. My dad's place was at the head of the room. My mom's place was on the sofa, praying with women and patting their backs. And I just assumed that when it came to ministry, *my place* was hiding in the hallway.

I was like a movie-goer with a front-row seat to Dad and Mom's work. I was so close to the action I could see things everyone else missed. But I wasn't really part of the show. Now I'll be honest, there were some perks to that! After all, life in the hallway was a lot more comfortable than life in the living room. In the living room people cried and talked about their problems and asked hard questions and endured awkward confrontations. In the hallway, all you had to do was lick your ice cream cone and watch.

Maybe you've never hidden in a hallway to spy on your parents' ministry, but in many ways this image captures MK life in a single snapshot. We are the constant observers, always watching but seldom belonging. In our host country, on the mission field, we don't look like everyone else. But in our parents' home country, we usually don't feel like everyone else. So we learn to live on the outside looking in. We learn to make mental notes everywhere we go so we can give off the appearance of fitting in. Take for instance the time I tried to join a gushing conversation about Brad Pitt (a major American celebrity) by casually asking if he was an upperclassman. *Note to self: Whoever Brad Pitt is, he's really hot, and he does NOT go to our school!* Or the time I tried to order McSpaghetti in Florida. *Note to self: McDonald's does NOT serve pasta in America!*

Give it enough time, and you can become really good at hiding in the hallway. You can become such a keen observer that you know how to blend in wherever you are. That was me. I learned early on how to navigate the different environments that tangled together to form my life, and eventually it got pretty comfortable. I learned to listen very carefully. I learned to read social cues. I learned to think before I spoke when on furlough. And I learned to breathe easy around fellow MKs, the one people group that truly understood me.

=====

But nothing prepared me for the day it all came crashing down. When I was 15 years old, my parents made the big announcement. Although my mom was from Singapore, my dad was born in the United States. And now we were leaving the Philippines—home—and moving to my father's native country.

Forever.

My older sister was graduating from high school, and my parents had requested a permanent stateside ministry placement so we could be nearby as she started college. It was as if someone pulled the plug on a gigantic bathtub, and just like that, I watched everything I knew swirl down the drain.

In the months to come, I read books about reentry shock and "third-culture kids." I tried to remember all the advice I had been given at MK conferences. At one point after returning to the United States, I even sat in a room with a counselor who made me draw pictures of places where I felt happy. It was helpful, but it wasn't enough. There was still this gaping ache in my heart. There was anger, confusion, sorrow, and fear all wrapped up in a big ball and glued together with bitterness. Somehow all the answers I received felt woefully inadequate.

Biblical counselor Deepak Reju once said, "Addressing the circumstances without addressing the heart is like offering a drink of water to a man who is on fire. It's not wrong; it's just insufficient." Oh, how I experienced the truth of that statement! I felt like a girl on fire, questioning the very character of God, while everyone handed me little cups of water filled with tips for how to make new friends. Don't get me wrong, I needed to make new friends. But I needed so much more than that! I needed more than lessons about culture and strategies for re-assimilation into the US.

I needed the big picture. I needed the comfort of the Master Plan, which alone can whisper into the heart, "There is a *purpose* for all of this!" Like a Google map, I needed to zoom out, to see that the story was bigger than me, and that it was worth all the suffering I would endure. That's why I'm writing this book. Because, dear MK, deep down, I believe that's exactly what you need too.

Before I get ahead of myself, let me pause and admit something I often longed to hear MK leaders admit to me: *I don't know you.* Being an MK is not like being a one-size-fits-all T-shirt. We are different. Not only do we have different experiences, we have different reactions to our experiences. We have different strengths, weaknesses, personalities, joys, and sorrows. Today, as I sit here thinking about you, I don't know if you were born an MK or became one later in life. I don't know if you speak five languages or one. I don't know if you live in a village or a booming metropolis, if you're homeschooled or president of your class. I don't know whether you love MK life, hate it, or don't give it a second thought. I don't know how you feel about God, your parents, or even yourself.

So when I say I know what you need, it's not because I'm psychic or because I think being an MK means I understand you completely. Rather, it's because the Bible reveals that despite our differences, all of humanity needs the same thing. We need the gospel of Jesus Christ.

This again? Whoa, whoa, whoa . . . hang on. We're missionary kids, remember? We hear about God ALL the time! What makes you think we need a better understanding of the gospel?

I get it. Really, I do. If I had a dime for every time I listened to my parents share their testimony in church, I'd drive a BMW. But there's a big difference between being exposed to the gospel and being changed by it. One of the greatest dangers of growing up as an MK is that the gospel can feel like that go-to meal your mom makes every week. Sure, it's good, but . . . *this again?* We foolishly believe we know all there is to know about it and, if we're honest, we might even admit it's kind of boring. Some of us were taught the gospel from such a young age that it tasted stale before it ever had a chance to taste fresh. So we missed it. Not necessarily an understanding of it, but an awe of it.

The first time I had the nagging sense that I lacked awe over the gospel, I was in college. I was also totally smitten with this cute Southern boy and his mile-long dimples. His name was Clint, and he was unlike me in every way. He was outgoing and popular; I was shy and, quite frankly, a nerd. He had a wild, ungodly past; I had a boring, squeaky clean one. He struggled to find Jesus; I exited the womb hearing stories about Jesus. You get the picture. But most of all, this cute boy (who would one day become my husband) was *passionate* about the gospel. And I was . . . not. He talked about Jesus and salvation like it still amazed him, like it was exciting and always relevant. The gospel wasn't part of his life; it was his life.

And it made me uncomfortable. I wasn't uncomfortable that the gospel meant so much to him. I was uncomfortable that it meant so little to me. After all, it was the same story! We had both been rescued by the same Savior. We both loved Him and wanted to live for Him. So why did the gospel taste like a feast to Clint, and like yesterday's ham sandwich to me? At first I thought it was because I knew the gospel too well. Because I'd dined on it too frequently. But actually, it was just the opposite. I hadn't dined on it nearly enough.

THE POWER OF THE GOSPEL

The Bible teaches us many things about the gospel. First and foremost, it teaches that the gospel *saves*. In a letter to the church in Rome, the Apostle Paul declared, "For I am not ashamed of the gospel, because it is the power of God that brings salvation to everyone who believes"

(Romans 1:16). Most of us know that the gospel saves, but we think that's all it does. The gospel saves us from hell, and then we try really hard to become more like Jesus, right? Wrong! The gospel doesn't just save us, it also *transforms* us.

Let me teach you two terms that will help keep things straight. Being saved happens in an instant. We receive Jesus as Lord, and we are made right with God. Theologians call this "justification." But becoming more like Jesus takes a lifetime. It is the daily practice of living like Jesus, which theologians call "sanctification." OK, ready for a challenge? See if you can spot *both* justification *and* sanctification in the following verse: "So then, just as you received Christ Jesus as Lord, continue to live your lives in him, rooted and built up in him, strengthened in the faith as you were taught, and overflowing with thankfulness" (Colossians 2:6–7).

Did you see it? Paul writes, "Just as you received Christ Jesus as Lord (justification), continue to live in him (sanctification)." Paul is basically saying, "Hey guys, how did you become Christians? Through the grace of the gospel, right? So let me tell you how to *live* as Christians . . . the very same way! Through the grace of the gospel."

The church in Galatia struggled with this concept. They realized they were saved by the gospel, but they were trying to grow as Christians through their own efforts. (I would've fit in well there!) Listen to the way *The Message* summarizes Paul's rebuke to them: "Let me put this question to you: How did your new life begin? Was it by working your heads off to please God? Or was it by responding to God's Message to you? Are you going to continue this craziness? For only crazy people would think they could complete by their own efforts what was begun by God. If you weren't smart enough or strong enough to begin it, how do you suppose you could perfect it?" (Galatians 3:2–3 *The Message*).

Ouch! OK, Paul, we get it—we don't just need the gospel for salvation; we need it every single day in order to become more like Jesus. But wait, there's more! The gospel saves us, transforms us, and also *compels* us. The more we dig into the gospel, the more we're motivated to share it with the world. In 1 Corinthians 9:16 Paul writes, "For when I preach the gospel, I cannot boast, since I am compelled to preach. Woe to me if I do not preach the gospel!" We are compelled to share the gospel, live in a manner worthy of the gospel, and endure persecution for the gospel. Ultimately, believers are compelled to be "striving together as one for the faith of the gospel" (Philippians 1:27), which is just a fancy way of saying we are called to *fight for it!*

But there's one big problem. We can't wage war from the hallway. No good soldier hides in the bushes to watch other men fight. He gets up and engages in the battle. But where do we find the courage and the power to do that?

We find the power to share the gospel *in* the very gospel itself! "For the message of the cross is foolishness to those who are perishing, but to us who are being saved *it is the power of God*" (1 Corinthians 1:18, author's emphasis). In other words, the gospel doesn't just compel us, it also *empowers* us. No wonder Paul constantly reminded believers of the gospel! We must do the same. We must remind ourselves of the gospel in every circumstance of our lives.

Humor me here for just a second. Let's pretend you have an evil twin who steals your identity and parades around in your place for months. Along the way, he (or she) destroys your reputation. He fails your exams, insults your friends, and loses your soccer game. When you finally figure out what's going on, how would you defend yourself? Would you say, "I'm sorry, guys. I was just having a bad day." Of course not! You would protest, "It wasn't me! You weren't interacting with the true me!"

If you find the gospel condemning, stifling, or irrelevant, *you probably aren't interacting with the true gospel*. It's possible you've been deceived by a counterfeit. And as Paul points out in Galatians, a false gospel is no gospel at all. Listen to what he writes: "I am astonished that you are so quickly deserting the one who called you to live in the grace of Christ and are turning to a different gospel—which is really no gospel at all" (Galatians 1:6–7). There is only one real gospel. It has the power to change your life and determine your eternal destination. Trust me: the stakes are too high to be fooled by a counterfeit.

In the next chapter we will unpack the true gospel, as revealed in the Bible. Throughout the remainder of the book we will examine how this gospel impacts your journey as an MK. But before you read on, pause and ask the Holy Spirit to help you understand the true gospel. Ask Him to rid you of misunderstandings, and invite Him to wow you with the truth. This is a prayer He delights to answer.

QUESTIONS FOR REFLECTION

"Hiding in the hallway" is an analogy for the feeling of being an outsider. As an MK, have you ever felt as if you didn't belong in your environment? What made you feel this way?

Do you feel a greater sense of belonging in your host culture (the country where your parents serve as missionaries) or in your home culture (the country of your or your parents' origin)?

What has been one of your best and worst experiences as an MK? Do you participate in your parents' ministry? If so, how?

At this point in your journey, do you believe you have a clear understanding of the gospel? Try to explain the gospel in three to four sentences.

Does the gospel ever seem boring, condemning, or unimportant to you? If so, why?

CHAPTER 2

HOW THE GOSPEL CHANGES EVERYTHING

When I attended MK conferences, one of my favorite pastimes was trading stories with other MKs about all the outrageous questions we'd been asked by non-MKs. *Do you live in a grass hut? Can you swing from trees? Have you ever seen a toilet?* Or my personal favorite: *Do you wear clothes?*

Just once, I wish I would've said, "Of course we do! I've got at least four loincloths back home." Can you imagine the conversation?

"Loincloths, really?!"

"Oh yeah! We make them out of caribou hide. Unless, of course, there's a shortage. Then we use small children. But not all of them. If we did that, we'd have nothing left for dinner!"

Please tell me times have changed and people today are a little less ignorant! For your sake, I hope so. Stumble your way through a few of those questions, and it doesn't take long to begin asking yourself, *what's the point?* What's the point of living overseas? What's the point of enduring the loincloth questions, or the "be-on-your-best-behavior" visits to a hundred different churches? What's the point of interrupting your life with a furlough every few years, or feeling like your own grandparents are strangers? *What's the point of being a missionary kid?*

In order to answer that question, I have to take you way back in time. Before you were born or your parents decided to be missionaries. Before Jesus died on the Cross. We have to travel all the way back to the beginning.

IN THE BEGINNING, GOD

When I was in college, I took a course called Bible for Teachers. The syllabus promised an overview of the entire Bible. On the first day of class, our professor told us to turn to Genesis 1:1. She read four words: "In the beginning God." Then she closed her Bible, and for the remainder of the hour, we talked about those four words. I remember thinking, *Good gracious! By the time we get to the Apocalypse it'll actually be taking place!* But my professor opened my eyes to a major theological truth that day: the story of the gospel doesn't start on a cross, or in a garden called Gethsemane. It starts at the very beginning, with God.

"In the beginning God." Think for a moment about the significance of those four words. From the dawn of time, in the very beginning, there was *God*. Notice, nobody created Him. *God has no beginning.* He has always existed. And I'm not just talking about God the Father. Genesis 1:2 says, "the *Spirit* of God was hovering over the waters" (author's emphasis), indicating that the Holy Spirit was also present from the very beginning. He too is timeless and eternal.

But what about Jesus? John 1:1–2 says, "In the beginning was the Word, and the Word was with God, and the Word was God. He was with God in the beginning." Verse 14 reveals that the "Word" is referring to Jesus Christ! Did you know that Jesus was present at creation? Since the Bible contains the account of Jesus' birth, it's easy to believe He only came into existence when Mary gave birth to Him. But as a member of the Godhead, Jesus Christ has always existed. Each person of our Triune God—Father, Son, and Holy Spirit—was present from the very beginning of time. *The Bible is His story.* It is the story of God, meant to reveal the character of God. The very first thing we learn about God is that He is Creator.

━━━━━━

Along with Bible for Teachers, I was also required to take an apologetics class in college. One morning our apologetics professor read us a short story. It was about two strangers who meet on an airplane and discuss faith in God. The narrative had been written by a student to convey principles from the course. Before long a heated debate sprang up regarding the characters in the story. What was their purpose? What was the author trying to convey? I listened with rapt attention as my peers argued back and forth. *"The purpose of the characters is this!"* *"No, no, it's that!"* *"The author created them to do this!"* *"No, that!"*

A grin spread across my face as I realized I was the only person in the classroom with the authority to end the debate. I alone could declare the purpose of those characters because I was the *author* of the story. That narrative was the final project I had submitted earlier in the week. Those characters belonged to me. I brought them to life. I didn't just *know* their purpose, I *dictated* their purpose. After all, the creator is the only one who has the right to determine the purpose of his creation.

In a passage asserting God's total sovereignty over man, Paul writes,

> But who are you, a human being, to talk back to God? Shall what is formed say to the one who formed it, "Why did you make me like this?" Does not the potter have the right to make out of the same lump of clay some pottery for special purposes and some for common use?
> —Romans 9:20–21

I can almost hear Paul saying, *"Of course He does!"* Of course the Potter has the right to make the pottery for whatever purposes He wants! He's the Potter, for crying out loud! But so many of us live as though we created ourselves. We parade around as if we have the right to determine the purposes for which we were made. What foolishness! The truth is we will never understand our purpose in this life unless we look to our Creator.

So why did God make us? The Bible teaches that God made you and me for a very simple but powerful purpose. To quote pastor David Platt, "We have been created to *enjoy* God's grace in a relationship with him" and "to *exalt*

God's glory to the ends of the earth." These two purposes actually go together, for the more we enjoy God the more we exalt Him. And as we exalt God, we come to realize that nothing in life is more enjoyable.

Let's try a little exercise. Read the following passage, and underline every example of the psalmist "enjoying" God. Look for expressions of his longing for God and satisfaction in God. Next, circle examples of the psalmist "exalting" God, or in other words, glorifying and praising God.

> You, God, are my God, earnestly I seek you; I thirst for you, my whole being longs for you, in a dry and parched land where there is no water. I have seen you in the sanctuary and beheld your power and your glory. Because your love is better than life, my lips will glorify you. I will praise you as long as I live, and in your name I will lift up my hands. I will be fully satisfied as with the richest of foods; with singing lips my mouth will praise you. —Psalm 63:1–5

Do you see the beautiful mingling of these two purposes? They flow seamlessly out of the psalmist's heart, one right on top of the other. At times it's hard to even differentiate between them. For instance, when the psalmist declares, "Your love is better than life," he is both exalting and enjoying God all at once. This is why we were made! To enjoy God. To exalt Him. Those are the only pursuits that will fill up all the empty spaces in our souls.

BORN WITH A PROBLEM

Once upon a time, two people knew what it was like to thoroughly enjoy and exalt God. Nothing held them back from their Creator. There was no sorrow, shame, warfare, or wickedness. You and I cannot even imagine such a world because it no longer exists. The moment Adam and Eve disobeyed God, they ushered the dominion of sin into the world. The Bible says that we *inherited* Adam and Eve's sinfulness (Romans 5:12; 1 Corinthians 15:21–22).

Imagine an unfaithful husband contracts HIV. He passes the virus to his wife, and she becomes pregnant. The tragic problem is not that their child may grow up and contract HIV through his own foolish choices. The problem is that their child will be *born* with HIV, having *inherited* the disease from his parents. Romans 5:12 tells us that "sin entered the world through one man [Adam], and death through sin, and in this way death came to all people, because all sinned." Just like a child who inherits a disease from his or her parents, you and I are destined to die because we have inherited the sinful nature of Adam. This is why the psalmist David cried out, "Surely I was sinful at birth, sinful from the time my mother conceived me" (Psalm 51:5).

How long do you think it takes for a child with HIV to begin manifesting symptoms of the disease? Doctors say not long. It's the same with us and our sin. We begin manifesting symptoms of our sin nature in record time. If you want proof, get a summer job babysitting toddlers. I guarantee by the time you and I were two years old, we were showing ample evidence of our sinfulness! And it hasn't stopped since. We lie, gossip, cheat, covet, envy, lust, and hate. In our hearts, we crave God's position and authority. We long to rule our own lives, to live for and exalt ourselves instead of Him.

———

Our sin spits in the face of God's perfect holiness. Because He is a just King, God hates sin. It is an intolerable abomination to Him. Think of it this way: a murderer kills a young mother. In one moment her entire family is devastated forever. Picture her parents, husband, and children huddling together on a courtroom bench. Nothing can bring this beloved woman back, but at least they can see justice served. The criminal enters the courtroom and all the evidence against him is presented. He's found guilty by the jury and sentenced to life in prison. Just as the family is hugging one another with relief, imagine the judge pounds his gavel and says, "Wait! You are guilty. But I am good. I'm dropping all charges against you. Go home—you're free!"

Do you feel sickened at the thought of this? How do you think the family would feel? Is the judge really *good*? Of course not! His lack of integrity is repulsive! To condone evil *is evil*, not good. Yet so many people believe that a "good" God should not sentence anyone to eternal punishment. If God followed this flawed definition of "goodness," He would be unjust and wicked. But God is the opposite. He is a perfectly holy Judge. Therefore, He cannot declare guilty sinners innocent. Proverbs 17:15 says, "Acquitting the guilty and condemning the innocent—the LORD detests them both."

THE BIG DILEMMA

But this means we have a big problem. How can God declare you and me innocent when we've already seen that we are guilty? We were born sinful, remember? What's more, we have acted on this sinful nature, committing millions of sins in our lifetime. If God forgives us without any penalty, He will be like the unrighteous judge!

So what did God do? He demanded a high penalty for sin . . . *then He paid the penalty Himself.* In this way, Jesus' death on the Cross not only saved humanity but also demonstrated God's character. The Cross is the voice of God crying aloud, "I am *holy,* for I punish sin! And I am *merciful,* for I bore the punishment Myself!" It is the perfect expression of justice and mercy.

But it came at an infinitely steep price. In order to pay the penalty for mankind's sin, God Almighty had to do two unimaginable things. First, He had to become human. The Bible says that Jesus Christ is the "image of the invisible God" (Colossians 1:15), the "radiance of God's glory and the exact representation of his being" (Hebrews 1:3). In other words, Jesus *is God*, yet He "made himself nothing by taking the very nature of a servant, being made in human likeness" (Philippians 2:7). Can you picture the God who built galaxies as a baby lying helplessly in a dirty diaper? Isn't it unfathomable? Could He have taken any form more defenseless and vulnerable? Yet Jesus Christ stooped down to this lowest degree. For the next 33 years, He led a sinless life despite extreme temptation and persecution. He revealed the glory and character of God as He served, taught, healed, rebuked, and worked wonders.

Then at just the right time, He did the second unimaginable thing. He took all of God's holy anger upon Himself. As Jesus died on the Cross, God showed Him no mercy. He poured the fullness of His wrath against sin onto Jesus. Imagine the sins of all humanity, past, present, and future. The judgment for all of that sin landed squarely on Jesus' shoulders. He didn't just experience the absence of God's grace on the Cross. Jesus experienced the presence of God's anger. He willingly endured it in order to demonstrate His character and to rescue you and me.

Among all the religions of the world no other god has ever done such a thing. The false gods of every other religion require mankind to *reach up to them* through meditation, rituals, or good works. But the one true God of the Bible *reached down*, in Christ, to rescue mankind. He came to us, because He knew we could never be good enough to come to Him. In the words of Isaiah 53:5, "But he was pierced for our transgressions, he was crushed for our iniquities; the punishment that brought us peace was on him, and by his wounds we are healed."

PUTTING ON YOUR SHADES

That's the gospel. The problem is, most of us grow up viewing this gospel like a get-out-of-hell ticket. We ask Jesus to come into our hearts, and we get a ticket to heaven. We shove it in our pocket and mostly forget about it. But the gospel is much more than a ticket to heaven. It's a way of life. It's a way of *viewing* life. It's not like a ticket; it's more like a pair of sunglasses. When you put on sunglasses, everything looks different. It's the same stuff, but it's *tinted* differently. The gospel is like that; it changes the way we look at the world. The way we look at our opportunities. The way we look at our friends, our problems, and our disappointments.

I want to teach you how to put on those sunglasses. I want to teach you how to view everything in your life through the lens of the gospel.

The furloughs and friendships and farewells. The culture shock and compassion. The loincloth questions. The experiences and adventures and heartaches. Believe it or not, the gospel has something to say about all of it.

QUESTIONS FOR REFLECTION

We were made to enjoy and exalt God. Would you describe yourself as someone who enjoys God? Why or why not?

Would you describe yourself as someone who exalts God? Why or why not?

Read Psalm 63:1–5 again. Can you relate to any of the emotions David expresses in this psalm? Which parts resonate with you, and which parts don't?

What are two new things you learned about the gospel in this chapter?

How does Jesus' death on the Cross demonstrate that God is both holy and merciful?

Do you treat the gospel more like a ticket to get out of hell, or like a pair of sunglasses through which you view every aspect of your life? What's the difference between the two?

CHAPTER 3

THE DANGER OF LIVING IN DAD AND MOM'S SHADOW

I smoothed my dress and tried to act normal, but inside my heart was hammering. It was the night of my older sister's high school graduation, and in the morning we were leaving the Philippines forever. The time had come to say goodbye to all my friends. I had dreaded this moment for months, but I attended enough MK seminars to know you're supposed to say goodbye well. What does that even mean, though? Does it mean you say it with a stiff upper lip? Or do you cry your eyes out so you can check "grieving" off the to-do list? *Say goodbye well!* I told myself. *The experts promise it's important. Maybe if you do it right, it won't hurt so much.*

Seventeen years later, it still sometimes hurts. In the end, I didn't shed a tear in front of my friends. I wanted to cry but couldn't. So I just told them how much I loved them, gave them a hug, and climbed into my family's minivan. Then I slammed the door, and in that one instant, I learned what it meant to have a broken heart. The grief didn't wash over me in waves, it exploded inside of me like a bomb. I sobbed and wailed and shook in the backseat of the van as though every friend I'd ever had was dead. To me, they might as well have been. I was moving 7,000 miles away, long before the days of social media and smartphones. But it wouldn't stop there. In the months to come, I would grieve more than just the loss of my friends. I would grieve the loss of security, familiarity, and, most of all, belonging. The loss of a world and a life that made sense. Relocating as a sophomore in high school didn't feel like the end of a chapter in my journey. It felt like the whole book had been tossed into a fire, and somehow from the ashes I was supposed to create a brand new life.

When it came to God, I walked a tightrope between love and hate for the next few years. I needed Him to survive. My beloved MK school of 600 students was gone, and soon I trod the corridors of a public high school with 2,000 students I neither knew nor understood. I no longer hid in my childhood hallway. Now I lurked in hallways where kids made out before class, screamed profanities, and told jokes I didn't understand. Once, in the middle of hallway "rush hour," I unknowingly walked along the wrong side of the hallway. I was like a fish swimming upstream until a large girl shoved me out of the way and called me a dirty name. I remember it because it was the first time I had ever been called that. From then on, I did what MKs do best. I watched and I learned. I walked on the right side of the hallway, I blended into the crowd, and I did my very best to become invisible.

During the day I clung to God, often imagining He held my hand. At night, when I curled up in bed and cried, I hated Him. I felt forgotten, betrayed, and, worst of all, like my whole life was one puny appendix stapled to the main story of my parents' ministry. God told them, "Go!" and I was dragged along. God told them, "Return!" and I was dragged along. It felt as if I were a stage prop in the play of their life.

THE ENGINE AND THE CABOOSE

Have you ever felt that way? I think it's a common MK feeling. The very term *missionary kid* describes us in light of our parents' vocation. They are missionaries. Therefore, we are the *kids of missionaries*. Their job is to make disciples of all nations, and our job is to tag along behind, right? Not exactly.

I promised to give you a gospel perspective of MK life, and the first thing you need to understand is that the gospel is personal. The call to know Jesus and to make Him known has not just been issued to your parents. It has been issued to *you*. There is something both comforting and challenging about this reality.

Here's the comforting part: because the gospel is personal, you are not just a stage prop in the play of your parents' lives. God is intimately acquainted with every detail of *your* life and every longing of *your* heart. He sees you, loves you, and has special plans just for you. Listen to the powerful words of Psalm 139:1–3, "You have searched me, LORD, and you know me. You know when I sit and when I rise; you perceive my thoughts from afar. You discern my going out and my lying down; you are familiar with all my ways."

David goes on to declare that God knew you long before you even existed. While He was weaving you together in the depths of the earth and placing you inside your mother's womb, He knew you. Verse 16 says, "Your eyes saw my unformed body; *all the days ordained for me* were written in your book before one of them came to be" (author's emphasis). Did you catch that? Not only does God know everything about you, He knows everything about your story. He knows every detail about every day you will ever live.

As MKs it's tempting to picture our parents as the engine of the train and ourselves as the caboose. We think God has a plan for their lives and we're forced to chug along behind. But that's not it at all! Picture instead the parallel sides of a railroad track. Imagine that one side represents God's will for your parents, and the other side represents His will for you. God's plans for each of you are unique, yet in His infinite sovereignty, He is able to weave these plans together so that they move in the same direction. There will come a day when those tracks diverge. As an adult, you will no longer be under your parents' authority. But before that time, as you move in line with your parents, you are in the very center of God's will for *you*.

When I finally grasped this truth—not just in my head but in my heart—it set me free. I had been living in the US for more than a year when I went outside early one morning to read a devotional. Something I read made me start to think about my life from God's perspective instead of my own. For the first time, I imagined how *God* must have felt as He planned the story of my life. He knew that when He ripped me away from the Philippines I would hate Him. He knew I would blame Him and sin against Him. But He did it anyway. He did it because He had plans for me, *good* plans for my future (Jeremiah 29:11). Like a loving parent, God acted in my best interest even though I kicked and screamed the whole way.

I was never invisible to Him. While I followed my parents in their missionary work, God was working out His plan and His will for *my* life. Sitting outside that morning, I repented. I remember whispering, "God, all along You loved me!" I still didn't know how God would use this trial in my life, but for the first time, I believed He had a purpose for *me* in this plan. And I believed His purpose was good.

What about you? Have you fallen prey to the engine/caboose mentality? Have you believed the lie that you don't matter to God? That your parents' ministry is center stage and you're just an afterthought? If so, it's time to look at yourself through the lens of the gospel. The gospel says the whole idea of you came from God. He designed you and brought you to life. Biologically, you are irreplaceable! In other words, there is only one you on the face of the planet. And you were God's idea, created for a one-of-a-kind purpose, a plan no one else can fulfill. The gospel goes on to reveal that God loves you so intensely, He died to redeem you. It says that in Christ you are holy, chosen, and beloved, called to a one-on-one relationship with God (Colossians 3:12). There is no such thing as a "caboose" when it comes to God's plans. Nobody was created to tag along behind. *The gospel is personal.*

———

I told you there was also a challenging aspect to this reality. Here it is: because the gospel is personal, *you* are accountable for how you respond to it. Romans 14:10–11 tells us that "we will all stand before God's judgment seat," and every single person will bow down and confess that Jesus is Lord. Verse 12 says, "So then, each of us will give an account of ourselves to God."

Dear MK, there will come a day when you must answer to the Holy Judge, and no one else can step forward for you. On that day you cannot hide behind your parents' faith or your pastor's faith or your best friend's faith. *The gospel is personal.* It is personally extended, and it must be personally received. This involves both faith and submission. It's kind of like strapping on a seatbelt. When you put on a seatbelt, you place your faith in something outside of yourself. You willingly submit to the seatbelt because you trust it; in fact, you stake your life on it. Yet even though it's a position of submission, it's deeply comforting. You're safe! You're secure. You're anchored in God's unbreakable love and sovereign will.

On the flip side, failing to receive the gospel is dangerous. When we believe the lie that the gospel is impersonal and we're just an afterthought to Dad and Mom's ministry, it naturally leads to bitterness. Left unchecked, this kind of resentment can estrange us from our parents. It can toughen our hearts so that we push others away. It can lead us to make foolish choices, sinning against God because we're mad at Him or hurt by Him. Nobody wins when we believe these lies! We grieve God's heart, and we're left wallowing in the sorrow and loneliness of our sin.

It doesn't stop there, though. Far more frightening is the reality that living in our parents' spiritual shadow impacts our eternal destination. When I finally joined the world of social media, while I found it great fun reconnecting with all my old MK friends, I was shocked to see how many had rejected Christianity. Don't get me wrong, I have former MK friends who are now passionately godly moms and teachers and artists and engineers. But 15 years ago, if you told me how many of my friends would one day abandon the faith, I would've said, "You're crazy!" Sadly, it has taken me years to realize that living in your parents' spiritual shadow is a real and *eternal* danger for MKs.

Remarkably, the danger can even extend beyond our own well-being. One of the toughest realities to face is that our lives impact other people. In other words, your decision to accept or reject the gospel affects more than just you. It affects the non-Christians passing through your life who may have questions about Jesus. It affects the younger siblings who want to be just like you. It affects the friends who are influenced by you and the parents who love you. One day, if you get married, it will affect the spouse building a life with you and the children who look up to you. When someone rejects Christ after a lifetime of learning about Him, it speaks loudly to a watching world.

AN HONEST PRAYER

If you're reading this, I imagine you're in one of three possible positions. You've either wholeheartedly accepted Christ, you've rejected Him, or you're not sure where you stand. In each possible scenario, I want you to know that you have hope. As long as there is breath in your lungs, you have hope! Jesus is bigger than our doubt, anger, apathy, or confusion. He is the God who holds the universe in the palm of His hand (Isaiah 40:12); our weakness does not scare Him. A heart that recognizes its own weakness is actually fertile soil for encountering Christ. So pause and be honest with Him. Tell God where you stand in relationship with Him, and tell Him where you *want* to stand.

There's a story in Mark 9:17–27 that demonstrates raw honesty before Christ. A father brings his demon-possessed son to Jesus and says, "If you can do anything, take pity on us and help us." Jesus notes his doubt: "'If you can'? said Jesus. 'Everything is possible for one who believes.' Immediately the boy's father exclaimed, 'I do believe; help me overcome my unbelief!'" (vv. 22–24).

It's as if the father were saying, "I admit I have doubts, but I *want* to believe You! Help me believe You." There's nothing wrong with a prayer like that. It's a prayer that recognizes our need for God, and the Bible promises God will never despise a humble, contrite heart that cries out for His mercy (Psalm 51:17).

The next two chapters will discuss some of the particular forms of suffering that can cause MKs to doubt or reject God. But before we go there, allow yourself time to reflect on your relationship with God. If it's helpful, use the following questions to dig deeper. It's not an overstatement to say that how you respond to Christ makes all the difference between life and death.

QUESTIONS FOR REFLECTION

Have you ever felt like an afterthought to your parents' ministry? What circumstances made you feel this way? Why is this sort of thinking dangerous?

Read Psalm 139:1–18. Which of these verses is the most comforting to you and why?

Think of a few people in your life who look up to you. How could your testimony of either following or rejecting Christ influence them?

In Matthew 12:30 Jesus makes a sobering statement. He says, "Whoever is not with me is against me, and whoever does not gather with me scatters." At this point in your life, would you consider yourself to be for or against Christ? Why? If you're not sure, explain what makes you uncertain.

If this chapter has raised questions about your standing before Christ, write down the name of one godly adult in whom you could confide. If possible, try to connect with him or her sometime this week.

CHAPTER 4

FORGING FRIENDSHIPS WITH SORROW AND SUFFERING

Several years ago, I started a book club in my home. One morning I sat in the living room with three friends to discuss the latest chapter of our book. I was looking forward to it because it was a chapter on suffering, and I was prepared for deep, soul-stirring conversation about our hardships in life.

Right from the get-go, my friend Melissa opened with a casual shrug. "You know, I really haven't gone through any pain in my life," she said. "I guess I've just had a pretty easy life."

I was dubious. "*Really?* Nobody ever dumped you?"

She shook her head.

"Made fun of you?"

"Not really."

"Ran over your pet dog?!"

"Nope."

I couldn't believe it. It's not like I parachute into war zones for a living, but I'm certainly no stranger to suffering. I know what it's like to be rejected, to lose something you really wanted, to watch people you love endure tragedies. When the other women in our book club shared that they too had encountered little pain in their lives, I realized the conversation was going to be skinnier than I had hoped.

Then one month later, the unthinkable happened. Melissa's one-year-old daughter pulled a cup of scalding coffee off the kitchen table, and it spilled all over her little body. She was rushed to a burn center two hours away with second-degree burns covering her face, shoulders, and stomach. For four days Melissa stayed in the hospital with her daughter while they performed numerous surgeries to remove dead skin. A few months after that nightmare, Melissa's young, healthy father was biking home from a deacon's meeting one afternoon when a car hit him. Melissa arrived at the scene of the accident in time to watch her father die, a sight that would give her nightmares for months. Finally, just as the dust started to settle, her mother was diagnosed with breast cancer.

If I was shocked when I thought Melissa hadn't experienced any suffering, I was speechless after watching the train wreck of pain unfold in her life. To be honest, I was afraid for her. How could someone who had never seen rain survive a tsunami? Why would God allow this? It just didn't make any sense.

Except that it did.

DON'T BE SURPRISED

To some extent every Christian should anticipate suffering. Why? Because the Bible promises it's coming. Shortly before Jesus went to the Cross He told His disciples, "In this world you will have trouble. But take heart! I have overcome the world" (John 16:33). Like it was for my friend Melissa, some of our suffering is the result of living in a broken world. Cancer will invade healthy bodies, impatient drivers will break the law, and human parents will forget to put the coffee out of reach. No doubt about it, this world is filled with trouble, and a portion of it is going to spill over into your life and mine. But there is another kind of suffering Christians are guaranteed to face, and that is the suffering that comes from following Christ.

For MKs, it can take on a thousand different forms. If your parents serve in an area that's hostile to the gospel, you may have encountered extreme persecution. I've heard stories about MKs whose homes have been robbed and whose parents have been kidnapped. I even know one MK whose father was killed for his faith. Sometimes the suffering is related to serving Christ in primitive locations. As a teacher, I taught MK twins whose dad contracted a disease overseas and died in the helicopter en route to the US for treatment.

Often the suffering isn't this extreme, but it's still confusing and painful. We find ourselves asking, *Why, God? Why do we have to move again? Why do we have to live in this place where there are only two TV channels in English? Why is it so hard to fit in when we go on furlough? Why couldn't I be there when Grandma died? Why would You call my best friend's family to another country? Why are my parents so stressed out? Why does raising support have to be so hard? Why does everybody have to stare at me everywhere we go?*

It feels astonishing. Our family gives up *everything* to tell others about Jesus, and *this* is the thanks we get?! But Peter tells us our attitude should be exactly the opposite: "Dear friends, do not be surprised at the fiery ordeal that has come on you to test you, as though something strange were happening to you. But rejoice inasmuch as you participate in the sufferings of Christ, so that you may be overjoyed when his glory is revealed" (1 Peter 4:12–13).

Wait, what?! Not only are we supposed to expect suffering, we're supposed to *rejoice* in it? Before you get carried away, let me tell you what this verse does not mean. It does not mean we're supposed to smile and say we feel great when secretly we want to burst into tears. Psalm 62:8 urges believers to honestly pour out their hearts to God because He is our refuge. There is no grief, anger, or depression He can't handle. When Peter instructs believers to rejoice when we participate in the sufferings of Christ, he isn't telling us to pretend we feel happy. Rather, he's urging us to recognize that there is value and purpose in suffering. But of course, the only way we'll see it is if we look through the lens of the gospel.

THREE PURPOSES OF SUFFERING

A few years ago, I traveled home to visit my mom and dad during a very painful season in my life. I felt shattered on the inside, and I didn't know how to deal with it. One day while perusing my parents' many (many!) bookshelves, I picked up a tattered copy of an old book by Hannah R. Hurnard called *Hinds' Feet on High Places*. It is the allegorical story of a girl named Much-Afraid who embarks on a journey to the High Places.

I read that book like I was starving and it was the last meal I was ever going to eat. I *was* Much-Afraid, desperate to journey to the Shepherd but weak and terrified. Of all the lessons I learned from that book, perhaps one of the most powerful was this:

GOD DESIGNS SUFFERING TO MAKE US MORE LIKE CHRIST

Just as Much-Afraid is about to set off on her journey, the Shepherd tells her, "I have most carefully chosen for you two of the very best and strongest guides." Much-Afraid is horrified to learn that the guides are named Suffering and Sorrow. But later in her journey, when the Shepherd asks her how she feels about them, this is what she says:

> I never could have believed it possible, Shepherd, but in a way I have come to love them. . . . They do truly want to get me up to the High Places, not just because it is the commandment which You have given them, but also because they want a horrid coward like myself to get there and be changed. You know, Shepherd, it makes a great difference in my feelings towards them not to look upon them any longer with dread, but as friends who want to help me.

Can you imagine viewing Sorrow and Suffering as *friends* who want to *help* us? It goes against every normal tendency in our hearts! Most people believe the ultimate goal in life is to be happy. In that case, suffering and sorrow are archenemies! But imagine the difference it would make in our attitudes if we quit viewing suffering and sorrow as enemies and instead embraced them as soul-shaping, character-building *guides*. As teachers designed to make us more like Jesus. Not only might we feel grateful for trials, we just may find ourselves *rejoicing* in the midst of them.

Listen to the way James puts it: "Consider it pure joy, my brothers and sisters, whenever you face trials of many kinds, because you know that the testing of your faith produces perseverance. Let perseverance finish its work so that you may be mature and complete, not lacking anything" (James 1:2–4). James isn't telling us to race around the house shrieking, "Hooray! We're moving, and I'm losing all my friends! What joy!" No, he's telling us to fix our eyes on the *fruit* this trial will bear in our lives. He's telling us to remember that God doesn't waste anything, least of all suffering. He uses it to accomplish His purposes, to make us more like Jesus.

I promise you, it is always hard when I encounter Sorrow and Suffering on my own journey. But they are the most excellent teachers I have ever known. And nothing is more encouraging than looking back over my life and realizing that, because of them, I am no longer the self-righteous girl I once was or the arrogant teenager or the idolatrous young adult. But that's not all! There are more purposes for suffering.

SUFFERING HAS THE POTENTIAL TO BRING GREAT GLORY TO GOD

Hebrews 11 talks about heroes of our faith who were tortured, stoned, sawed in two, homeless, destitute, and persecuted. Pause for a moment, and reread that list. *(Sawed in two?!)* That is *extreme*, unthinkable suffering. If you have the time, open your Bible and read Hebrews 11 for yourself. Each of these heroes of the faith clung to the promises of God, even when the promises were not yet fulfilled. The Bible says their "weakness was turned to strength" and "the world was not worthy of them" (Hebrews 11:34, 38). Thousands of years later, their testimonies of faithfulness in the face of suffering are still bringing glory to God! Imagine how *your* testimony could glorify God as you choose to follow Him in spite of suffering.

In a sermon, I once heard pastor Louie Giglio refer to our attitudes during times of suffering as a "megaphone." You know, those big cone-shaped things cheerleaders hold to their mouths? It makes their voices boom across rowdy stadiums. That's what suffering is like. It catches everyone's attention. It booms the gospel over the loudspeakers of life. Louie talked about a teenage girl in the audience who was dying of cancer yet joyfully in love with Christ. Her cancer had become a megaphone for God's glory.

What megaphones are in your life right now? What obstacles could become platforms for sharing the hope of the gospel? People are curious about how others handle suffering. They turn to watch. Suffering is an opportunity to put "feet" to our faith. It's an opportunity to "live out" our salvation as God works in us according to His good purpose (Philippians 2:12–13).

SUFFERING IDENTIFIES US WITH CHRIST

Finally, suffering *for* Christ identifies us *with* Christ. It identifies us as belonging to Him. Did you notice that the two Bible verses we examined about suffering both link "suffering" with "testing"? Look at them again:

> Dear friends, do not be surprised at the fiery ordeal that has come on you *to test you*, as though something strange were happening to you. —1 Peter 4:12 (author's emphasis)

> Consider it pure joy, my brothers and sisters, whenever you face trials of many kinds, because you know that the *testing of your faith* produces perseverance. —James 1:2–3 (author's emphasis)

Suffering tests our faith. It forces our hearts to answer questions like: "Am I going to keep trusting God? Do I really believe God is worth everything? Am I willing to praise Him even when it hurts? Will I believe His character is good even when my circumstances are bad?" When we say "yes!" to these questions, not just with our mouths but with our *lives,* we grip that megaphone and bring booming glory to God! We show the world we truly belong to Christ. We are *in* Him and He is *in* us! He is supernaturally working within us to produce fruit we could never produce on our own.

But it gets even better. Those who identify with Christ in His suffering also get to identify with Him in His *glory*! It makes me think of the children's folk tale about the little red hen. Do you remember that story? The little red hen works so hard to plant and harvest her grain, to mill it into flour, to bake the flour into bread. At each stage she asks the other farm animals, "Who will help me plant my grain? Who will help me cut the wheat? Who will help me grind the flour?" Every time, the other animals say, "Not I!" On and on she asks, until at last the bread is baked and the wonderful smell wafts out to the barn. When the hen asks, "Who will help me eat my bread?" they all cry, "I will!" But it's too late. She eats it all by herself.

The lesson is very simple: you don't get the reward without the labor. Think for a moment of the biggest trial in your life right now. Maybe it's huge; maybe it's small. It may be directly related to following Christ, such as persecution by peers for the wise choices you make or moving because of your parents' missionary work. Or maybe it's not directly related to following Christ, like my friend Melissa whose daughter was burned, but it's still a test of your faith. Imagine that Jesus looks at you and says, "Who will endure mockery for Me? Who will worship Me even if he loses his friends? Who will give up her comfortable life for My sake? Who will . . . [fill in the blank]?" Fill it in with your trial.

There are only two answers. You can say, "I will!" Or you can say, "Not I!" When it's time for the reward, those two answers will make all the difference in the world. Look one last time at our key verse: "Dear friends, do not be surprised at the fiery ordeal that has come on you to test you, as though something strange were happening to you. But rejoice inasmuch as you participate in the sufferings of Christ, *so that you may be overjoyed when his glory* is revealed" (1 Peter 4:12–13, author's emphasis).

Do you see how suffering is linked to glory? Why do we rejoice in the face of suffering? Because one day all true disciples of Jesus will also share in His glory! As Paul once wrote to his young protégé Timothy, "Here is a trustworthy saying: If we died with him, we will also live with him; if we endure, we will also reign with him. If we disown him, he will also disown us; if we are faithless, he remains faithful, for he cannot disown himself" (2 Timothy 2:11–13).

OK, let's be gut-level honest for a minute. While each of these beautiful purposes makes suffering *valuable*, they still don't make it *easy*.

Suffering is always difficult, and there may be times when you and I fail to embrace it biblically. There may be times when God asks, "Who will endure this for Me?" and we cry, "Not I!" Think of Peter. He loved Jesus, but he still denied even knowing Jesus three times. He was unwilling to suffer for Christ. But when Peter was faithless, Christ remained faithful. Why? Because Jesus cannot deny His own character. He is always faithful.

Years later, through God's work alone, Peter became the man that Jesus always knew—and even prophesied—he would be. Peter boldly proclaimed the gospel and was willing to be crucified (tradition says upside down!) for Christ's name. *That's what God can do in a life!* That's what God can do in *your* life. He can turn fear into courage, suffering into glory, doubt into faith. Remember, one of the most fundamental truths of the gospel is that we do not save ourselves. We need a Savior not only to rescue us from hell, but to make us more like Jesus every single day.

QUESTIONS FOR REFLECTION

There's a difference between suffering because we live in a broken world and suffering as a result of following Christ. Read the examples below, and write "world" beside examples of suffering as a result of our broken world, and "Christ" beside examples of suffering for following Christ:

_____ Being diagnosed with a rare illness.

_____ Having a hurricane damage your home.

_____ Being ridiculed because you won't watch an inappropriate movie.

_____ Losing a loved one.

_____ Having to live on a tight budget because your family serves overseas.

_____ Being reprimanded for talking about your faith at school or work.

Have you ever suffered as a result of following Christ? If so, how?

How can Christians view sorrow and suffering as friends or teachers rather than enemies?

Reread 1 Peter 4:12–13 and James 1:2–3. In your own words, explain the connection between "suffering," "testing," and "glory."

What are three purposes for suffering? Which one impacts you the most and why?

Think of a current trial you are facing or a recent trial you have faced. Talk to God about how you responded to it. If necessary, ask Him to forgive you for your wrong responses and help you become the person He wants you to be.

CHAPTER 5

UNDERSTANDING FOUR COMMON MK STRUGGLES

I rolled my eyes. Michael was at it again. Every day I listened to him exchange dirty jokes with the guys around him. Unfortunately, my assigned seat in economics class was directly behind Michael, so I was stuck listening to him whether I wanted to or not. But today was different. Today the subject of his crude talk was a close friend of mine. At last I couldn't stand it any longer.

"Will you please just stop?" I blurted. They were the first words I'd ever spoken to Michael. A strange look came over his face. Anger? Embarrassment? To this day, I still don't know exactly what he was feeling. But he stopped talking. Two class periods later a girl ran up to me.

"Jeanne, *what on earth* did you do to Michael?!"

I stopped dead in my tracks, a sick feeling in my stomach. "Why?"

"He's putting you on his website," she said.

Everyone knew about Michael's website. It was a gossip ring, as juicy and R-rated as any tabloid. Only Michael's "celebrities" didn't roam red carpets; they walked the halls of our school. Being featured on his website meant that in less than 24 hours, everyone would be whispering about you behind your back.

I silently vowed I wouldn't visit the website, no matter what. I didn't want to know what Michael was going to write about me. But I was scared. I went home and told my mom, "I think I'm in big trouble."

That night as my stomach churned in bed, part of me wished I had just laughed along with Michael's dirty jokes. Then he wouldn't be threatening to put me on his website. For the first time in my life, I actually felt *persecuted* for following Christ. And it made me angry. I was angry at Michael, of course. But I was also angry at God. *Why are You letting this happen?* I wanted to shout. *I did the right thing! I stood up for my friend! Why are You allowing me to become the laughingstock of the whole school?* It felt so unfair.

FOUR WAYS MKS SUFFER

In the previous chapter we talked about three purposes of suffering. I challenged you to embrace suffering as a teacher, to use it as a platform to glorify God, and to anticipate the reward ahead. In this chapter, I want to get down to the nitty gritty. How do you actually live that out? What do you tell yourself every single day when you're faced with real heartache?

Let's examine four of the most common ways MKs suffer. As we do, we'll ask ourselves the question, "How can I view *this trial* in light of Jesus' life, death, and resurrection?" That's what it means to have a gospel perspective of suffering.

1. FEELING ROOTLESS

"Rootlessness" could easily be identified as the hallmark of MK suffering. In the 1960s Dr. Ruth Hill Useem coined a term to describe kids like us. She called us Third Culture Kids (TCKs), suggesting that the act of being raised in a foreign culture causes a child to create a third culture, which is a blend of the home and host culture. For instance, if your parents are American and you're raised in Australia, your third culture is an American-Aussie blend. It exists only to your family and the fellow missionary families who share your experience. While TCKs embrace attributes of both cultures, they never fully identify with any culture. It's the reason we all take a deep breath before answering the question, "So where are you from?" We're not really "from" any one place. We're rootless.

The first thing the gospel teaches us about the pain of feeling rootless is that Jesus felt it too. In Matthew 8:20 He says, "Foxes have dens and birds have nests, but the Son of Man has no place to lay his head." Jesus knows exactly what it's like to be a stranger in a foreign land. He knows what it's like to be nomadic, to never fully be "part" of the world in which you live. Moreover, Jesus *chose* the pain of rootlessness for our sakes.

Have you ever thought about the fact that Jesus could've stayed in heaven? I'm pretty sure He fits in perfectly there. In fact, the Bible describes heaven as a place where Jesus is worshiped and exalted constantly (Revelation 5:11–12). It is the only place where Jesus is treated *exactly* how He deserves to be treated. But Jesus allowed Himself to be "uprooted." He came to a world where He would never fully be understood or accepted. A world that would despise and murder Him. Why? To save humanity and give us a picture of God's heart. Dear MK, as Jesus asks you to endure rootlessness for His sake, remember, He did it first for your sake.

But that's not all the gospel teaches us. When Jesus reconciled us to God through the Cross, He gave us the promise of a future home with Him in heaven (2 Corinthians 5:8). And guess what? Jesus isn't the only one who fits in perfectly in heaven. We will too. In his book, *In Light of Eternity*, author Randy Alcorn describes it like this:

> *Home* as a term for heaven is not simply a metaphor. It describes an actual, physical place—a place built by our bridegroom, a place we'll share with loved ones, a place of fond familiarity and comfort and refuge, a place of marvelous smells and tastes, fine food and great conversation, of contemplation and interaction and expressing the gifts and passions God has given us. . . . And, incredibly, the longing of the Carpenter-King—he who holds the title deed to heaven—is that we should join him as his beloved bride and live with him there forever.

I love that description! Years ago, as a young MK, I underlined those words with tears in my eyes. You see, I have always longed for *home* . . . it just took me a while to realize I wasn't longing for an earthly home, but a heavenly one. Ecclesiastes 3:11 says God has "set eternity in the human heart," meaning it's normal for us to crave a "forever place" of belonging.

When we long for a place to belong, we are actually longing for our eternal home with Jesus. So how do we deal with feeling rootless on earth? We pour out our hearts to Jesus, the One who really gets it. And we remind ourselves that there will come a day when we are finally *home* in the deepest, most satisfying sense.

2. SACRIFICING PHYSICAL COMFORTS

Another common form of suffering for MKs is foregoing physical comforts. The first winter I spent as a sophomore in the US, I nearly froze to death. *In Florida.* Kids at school constantly made fun of my Rudolph-nose, which was basically red from November until April. After a few winters my body finally acclimated . . . just in time for a visit back to the Philippines. I literally could not stop sweating. I could be standing still, under a fan, in a tank top, and sweat would be rolling down my temples. Not to mention all the street-side food I grew up eating suddenly made me violently sick. One afternoon, when I was sweating like a pig and throwing up *again*, I decided to take a shower. I walked into the bathroom and saw a gigantic bucket of water with a little scooper. I don't know why it surprised me— for 15 years I had bathed this way. There was never a working showerhead or bathtub in my childhood home. I would just sit on a little stool and dump water over myself with the scooper. But that day as I huddled in the bathroom, dumping cold water over my sticky, nauseated body, all I could think was, *"How did I ever LIVE like this?!"*

Can you relate? Have you ever made The List? You know, that list of all the physical comforts you're sacrificing as an MK? The list of all the things you're going to do and eat and buy and watch when you visit your home country? (Visit Grandma, eat Lucky Charms, buy an American Girl doll, and watch Saturday morning cartoons . . . that was my list in fifth grade.) If you've grown up on the mission field, The List may not be a big deal to you. But for kids who become MKs later in life, the loss of these basic comforts can feel brutal. So what does the gospel have to say about sacrificing physical comforts?

The gospel reminds us that no sacrifice we ever make for Christ will outweigh the sacrifices He made for us. Jesus didn't take on a third-world country; He took on the confines and limitations of humanity. He didn't give up cable TV, central air-conditioning, and Snickers bars; He gave up the right to His glory and power, making "himself nothing by taking the very nature of a servant" (Philippians 2:7). He sacrificed His dignity when He allowed others to spit in His face, beat Him up, make fun of Him, and nail Him to the Cross. He sacrificed His Father's pleasure when He accepted God's wrath on our behalf.

The gospel also teaches us that true disciples must be willing to follow Christ's example. We must be willing to give up *everything*. Matthew 16:24 says, "Then Jesus said to his disciples, 'Whoever wants to be my disciple must deny themselves and take up their cross and follow me.'" And yet, in so doing, we actually *gain everything!* In the next verse, Jesus goes on to say, "For whoever wants to save their life will lose it, but whoever loses their life for me will find it" (v. 25).

I promise there is a reward coming for true followers of Christ, and it will be so much better than cable TV or central air-conditioning. The more we adopt a gospel perspective of our circumstances, the more we will view each sacrifice as an offering of love and worship for a worthy King.

3. LIVING IN A FISHBOWL

A third hardship MKs face is fishbowl syndrome. Have you ever heard the expression "living in a fishbowl"? It means being on display. After all, nobody cuddles a fish or plays fetch with it, right? Fish are meant to be looked at, and sometimes it feels like MKs are too. Blonde hair in Zimbabwe? *Fascinating!* Blue eyes in Thailand? *Wow!* Weird accent? Social faux pas? Freckles?!

Suffice it to say, we tend to stand out. Sometimes being watched in our host culture is endearing. If you've ever had small children reverently stroke your hair or arms, you know how sweet it can be. They marvel at how different you are, and their wonder reflects the genius of our Creator.

He paints innumerable shades of skin! He speaks thousands of languages! He is the God of the world!

But sometimes being watched may feel irritating. It's one more sign that we're different. Have you ever been called to the front of a classroom or church auditorium so someone could announce that your parents are m-i-s-s-i-o-n-a-r-i-e-s? Dozens of eyes stare at you like you might spontaneously sprout a horn on your head. *I wonder if they're going to make me recite the whole Bible or do an impromptu tribal dance. Awkward!*

What does the gospel have to say about being on display? For starters, *it's OK not to fit in.* As a matter of fact, it's preferable. Remember, earth is not our home. We're not meant to slip in seamlessly here. All Christians are called to identify with Christ in ways that set us apart. So thank God for the unique ways you get to be set apart for Him. Moreover, thank Him for the red hair and freckles that nobody in rural Indonesia has ever seen before! Remember, He created you! What's different to them is beautiful to *Him.*

4. LEAVING LOVED ONES

A fourth (and perhaps the most painful) hardship MKs endure is saying goodbye. Do you want to know an honest confession? Even as an adult, it still stings sometimes. I was 20 years old when I started dating my husband. One weekend he took me to his hometown and introduced me to everyone. I saw his childhood home, schools, and favorite hangout spots. In the months to come, I got to know his friends pretty well. I went on trips with them, listened to them reminisce, and eventually attended most of their weddings.

Surprisingly, at times it really *hurt.* It hurt because I realized I couldn't show Clint my world. I couldn't make him understand. Even if I spent my last dime to buy crazy-expensive plane tickets to the Philippines, most of my friends were long gone. After graduation, they spread across the globe to attend college and get on with their lives. When I left my world, I left it forever.

I've often wondered if social media would've made it easier or harder. When I was a teenager there was no such thing as Facebook, Twitter, or

Instagram. As a matter of fact, dinosaurs still roamed the earth. . . . OK, just kidding! I'm not *that* old! But social media simply didn't exist. On one hand, I imagine I would have enjoyed the opportunities social media provides for keeping up with friends. On the other hand, watching my friends on a smartphone or laptop probably would've felt like slowly peeling off a Band-Aid—instead of moving on and making friends in my new location, I might have spent all my time living a virtual life by means of technology.

I got a small taste of how it might have felt when I finally did create a Facebook page in my twenties. Of course, I friended all my old MK buddies, which was great fun. Then one day I stumbled upon a picture one of them had posted. It was an old snapshot of a formal high school event, taken after I had left. I saw all my friends dressed up, with their arms around one another, laughing at some inside joke. The pain was as swift and sharp as a slap. In that moment I realized that while I was sitting in a cafeteria by myself, struggling so hard to fit in halfway across the world, they were laughing and making memories together. A million memories without me. Of course, on some level I *knew* they were moving on without me. But I didn't have to *see* it. I didn't have to see how much saying good-bye had cost me. Being a missionary kid had cost me so much.

When it comes to this form of suffering, the Bible issues a mighty promise: "'Truly I tell you,' Jesus replied, 'no one who has left home or brothers or sisters or mother or father or children or fields for me and the gospel will fail to receive a hundred times as much in this present age . . . and in the age to come eternal life'" (Mark 10:29–30).

A hundred times as much?! That's quite a reward! It's almost like Jesus is saying, "Look, I get it. I'm asking you to sacrifice a lot for Me. But you have to understand, what I'm asking you to give up is a dust mite compared to all that I will give you in return!"

Precious MK, when God calls us to leave beloved people or places, He *rewards* our obedience. Hold that truth in your heart when it hurts the most!

Sometimes the reward isn't what we expected, but it's always the very best reward. When I left the Philippines, I hoped God would reward me with oodles of friends, popularity, and an easy transition. But looking back, I realize He gave me a far more valuable and lasting reward: He used my trials to deepen my character. He didn't give me the fleeting gift of popularity. He gave me perseverance and spiritual maturity, gifts I could carry for the rest of my life.

But notice, Jesus didn't just promise earthly rewards. He promised the future reward of eternal life. Again, we see that a gospel perspective of suffering always lifts our eyes to the eternal. This is the Christian's greatest hope. In Christ, we can endure any and all earthly suffering because we know that "our light and momentary troubles are achieving for us an eternal glory that far outweighs them all" (2 Corinthians 4:17).

WHAT HAPPENED WITH MICHAEL'S WEBSITE

Are you beginning to see a common theme? A gospel perspective of suffering always turns our eyes toward Jesus as our sympathizer and eternity as our hope. No wonder Peter concludes, "So then, those who suffer according to God's will should commit themselves to their faithful Creator and continue to do good" (1 Peter 4:19).

In the end, that's what I did with the website crisis. As I lay in bed, agonizing over what Michael would write about me, I committed myself to my faithful Creator. I put my future and my reputation in His hands, and I resolved that I would continue to follow Him, no matter what. My parents also prayed. In fact, my mom sent an email to several close friends asking them to pray for me.

At school the next day, I braced myself for the onslaught. I knew I would hear about what was on the website whether I wanted to or not. But by lunchtime nobody had said a word about it. I finally approached the same friend who first told me about Michael's intentions. "Didn't Michael write about me on his website?" I asked.

"No," she said. "I heard Brandon talked him out of it."

Brandon? He was Michael's friend, a tall, skinny guy in my creative writing class who rarely smiled and always wore black. Like, head-to-toe black. *Brandon talked him out of it?!* I couldn't believe it! I barely knew

Brandon, but because I loved Jesus I was always kind to him—willing to partner with him in class when no one else wanted to and quick to compliment his writing when I liked it. Wouldn't you know, my faithful Creator used this unlikely character to rescue me.

Sometimes this is the way God chooses to work. As we entrust ourselves to Him, He rescues us out of the suffering. And sometimes, He rescues us *through* the suffering. Sometimes nothing changes . . . except us. Do you remember my friend Melissa and her intense season of suffering? Her daughter's burns, her father's death, and her mother's breast cancer? God didn't instantaneously heal Melissa's daughter or her mother. He didn't resurrect her father back to life. But He did resurrect Melissa's faith. He used suffering to draw her closely and intimately to Himself. If we commit ourselves into the hands of our faithful Creator, He will do the same for us.

QUESTIONS FOR REFLECTION

This chapter discusses four common forms of suffering for MKs: feeling rootless, sacrificing physical comforts, living in a fishbowl, and leaving loved ones. Which of these has been the hardest for you? Why?

How can Jesus relate to feeling rootless? How was His experience even more intense than ours?

What are some of the things you have had to sacrifice as an MK? How do you feel about not having these things?

Why is it OK *not* to fit in? Use a Bible verse to support your answer.

Do you believe social media has made it easier or harder to leave friends and loved ones? Explain.

Think about a trial you are currently facing. Now think about the gospel. How might Jesus be able to understand some of the things you are feeling?

CHAPTER 6

DEALING WITH THE DARK SIDE OF MINISTRY

When I was young, I took ballet lessons at one of the largest dance academies in Asia. It was called the Halili Cruz School of Ballet, and it was the closest thing to a castle I have ever seen. Each week hundreds of girls spun across the shiny wooden floors, filling the academy with pliés and pirouettes.

In case you're wondering, I never quite fit in. For starters, I was basically the class giant—a whole head taller than the Filipino girls my age. To make matters worse, I didn't speak the language, so I had to rely solely on nonverbal cues to make sense of anything. It worked well enough on ordinary days when we followed a routine. But every now and then, I would show up for class and discover we were taking an exam, or it was picture day and all the moms were putting makeup on their little ballerinas while my dad and I stared at each other awkwardly.

Recitals were the worst. Nothing was predictable. For that reason, I usually avoided them altogether. But one year we were performing *Alice in Wonderland*, and my class was cast as daisies, and for some reason I wanted to participate. So they fitted me for an extra-large daisy costume, and I started attending rehearsals at a theater in the Philippines. On opening night my family sat in the audience and watched the show. They told me it was beautiful. Mesmerizing! Elegant! Flawlessly graceful!

But I wasn't in the audience. I was backstage . . . and backstage it was nuts! Most of the dancers had to perform several different routines, and the minute they glided behind the curtain, they ripped their costumes off and sprinted to their dressing rooms. They tripped over wires, hissed at crew members, tore feathers off their heads, and fastened on tiaras in clouds of hairspray. It was glittered-and-sequined insanity! On stage the dancers were goddesses, and backstage they were gluing on fake eyelashes and screaming for safety pins. On stage they floated like fairies, and backstage they barked like rabid dogs.

MINISTRY AND "THE DARK SIDE"

It's a little disenchanting, isn't it? Seeing the *other* side . . . the side behind the curtain. When you're sitting in the audience, the life of a missionary family can look picture perfect. Noble, rewarding, even inspiring. But you and I get to see the fake eyelashes. We see the sweating and sighing and sobbing that goes on backstage when no one else is watching.

Sometimes we may not know *exactly* what's going on, but we know something's wrong. There has to be a reason Dad is so stressed out and Mom's eyes are red when we get home from school. Maybe we catch snippets of conversation, enough to puzzle together pieces of the conflict or crisis. When we're older, sometimes our parents will fill us in completely: they haven't raised adequate financial support . . . there's a dispute among team members . . . the head of our ministry is stepping down . . . policies are changing that will impact our lifestyle . . . we're being reassigned . . . Dad's leadership is being criticized . . .

It's incredibly unsettling. The first time I learned people were critical of my father, I felt a whirlwind of emotions. I was embarrassed. I felt *guilty* for being embarrassed. I felt loyal and sympathetic for my dad, but I also felt confused and anxious. The first time I saw my mom's feelings get hurt in ministry, it was equally disturbing. How do we respond to the dark side of ministry? The painful and confusing side? As we continue looking through the lens of the gospel, we'll see three truths: ministry is a gift, ministry is a mess, and God is in control of it all.

THE PRICELESS GIFT OF MINISTRY

If you'll remember back to chapter 2, the gospel begins with God creating us to enjoy and exalt Him. In other words, we have *purpose*. We were made to worship God. Don't gloss over this truth! When something is made for a purpose, it will never be useful or satisfied until it fulfills that purpose.

Have you ever picked up an object in your mom's kitchen and been like, "What *is* this thing?" There are some strange-looking objects in kitchen drawers, right? They have pointy parts, sharp parts, rubber flappy parts . . . it's weird! But then your mom will grab it and say, "Oh! That's my lemon juicer," and she'll take a fat lemon, grind it over the top of that weird plastic object, and suddenly all the juice is collected in the bottom and the seeds are trapped in a little tray. Genius! Every single part of that juicer was carefully designed for one purpose—juicing a lemon. If you don't know the purpose, the tool is useless. But if you *do* know the purpose, it's brilliant.

You and I are like that. We have been *carefully designed* for a purpose. Our hearts long to worship our Creator God. When we stumble upon this purpose, our soul sings with the brilliance of it. If you've ever worshipped God, you've probably experienced what I'm talking about. Maybe you were in an auditorium singing praises, and your spirit filled with joy. Or you were praying earnestly, and peace washed over you. Or as you read the Bible, your mind suddenly understood what you were reading, and your heart whispered, *Yes!* Have you ever felt that way before? When we do what we were made to do, something inside just feels right! The pieces click together, and joy streams out of our hearts like lemon juice.

So what does this have to do with your family's role as missionaries? In his book *Let the Nations Be Glad!* pastor John Piper writes, "Missions is not the ultimate goal of the church. Worship is. Missions exists because worship doesn't." Think about that for a moment. Why are families like yours traveling to the ends of the earth? So that the whole world might worship God! Your family is spreading the truth about mankind's purpose! They're teaching others to worship Jesus and, in so doing, to find the greatest joy and fulfillment imaginable.

Getting to be part of this work is a gift! Have you ever thought about the fact that God doesn't need your help? Everything your family is doing overseas, God could do by Himself in an instant. But He is allowing you the honor and joy of being part of His kingdom work.

OK, so if it's such an honor and joy, why does it sometimes get so ugly? Keep looking at ministry through the lens of the gospel. What comes next? After God created us to worship Himself, mankind sinned. Talk about a game-changer! Now everything—*everything*—has been touched by the Fall. That means ministry is done by sinful people, working with other sinful people, under the leadership of sinful people, in order to reach sinful people. That's quite a lot of sin in a tight space! Suffice it to say, there are a lot of ways to be hurt and to hurt others in ministry. Let's start with two of the most important people in your life, who may have inadvertently hurt or confused you along the way.

WHEN DAD AND MOM MESS UP

Do you remember the first time you realized your parents weren't perfect? The first time you heard one of them say a curse word? Or explode in anger and have to apologize later? Chances are you were pretty young. (I know my kids were!) Even if you grow up knowing your parents are sinners saved by grace, it's still hard to see them mess up.

Perhaps they start venting one day, and suddenly you know way more about church leaders than you ever should have known. Or maybe they smile for everyone else but wear their discouragement like a wet blanket the moment they walk through the front door. Maybe they complain or lose their temper or fight regularly. Maybe they've turned ministry into an idol, so it's all they think, talk, or worry about.

What are you supposed to do? The Bible provides several principles for how sons and daughters should interact with their parents. Ephesians 6:2 says, "Honor your father and mother." This is where you must start. Everything you say to your parents (or *about* your parents) should be characterized by respect. Your attitude and actions toward them should be honorable. If you believe they're sinning, so you scream at them or gossip about them, you've jumped straight into sin alongside them. Listen to the way Jesus put it:

> Why do you look at the speck of sawdust in your brother's eye and pay no attention to the plank in your own eye? How can you say to your brother, "Let me take the speck out of your eye," when all the time there is a plank in your own eye? You hypocrite, first take the plank out of your own eye, and then you will see clearly to remove the speck from your brother's eye. —Matthew 7:3–5

Whenever God burdens you to confront someone about an area of sin in their life, step one is making sure your own heart is right with God. So before talking to your parents, talk to God. Confess any sin and ask Him to fill you with humility, recognizing that He has given your parents authority over you, not vice versa. You may not even know what to pray for your parents, but guess what? The Holy Spirit does! Romans 8:26 promises that He is always praying for the saints according to God's will. So join Him in prayer, inviting Him to use you however He pleases and to show you the right time to talk with your parents.

When the opportunity presents itself, share your heart with them humbly and graciously. Ephesians 4:2–3 says, "Be completely humble and gentle; be patient, bearing with one another in love. Make every effort to keep the unity of the Spirit through the bond of peace." In other words, don't start with fighting words. Start with a gentle tone of voice. Express what you saw or heard and how it made you feel. You might say something like, "Mom, yesterday when you talked about Pastor Tim, I felt confused. You taught me to respect Christian leaders, but what you said about him wasn't kind." Or you might say something like, "Dad, I've noticed you seem stressed about money lately, and it makes me feel worried. You've always taught me that God will provide for us, but it doesn't seem like you're trusting Him."

You would be amazed at the way God can use you in your parents' lives. My mom still tells others that she learned to be grateful for our house because I confronted her when I was just a teenager. To be honest, I didn't even pray or seek to be humble—I was just so sick of her complaining that I finally said something. But God used it to work in my mom's life, and because of *her* humility, it bore fruit.

Another time when I think it's crucial to talk to your parents is when you feel misunderstood. Your parents may not be sinning, but it's possible they don't realize how much a decision is impacting you. For instance, because I went to one of the largest MK schools in Asia, I grew up with a lot of MKs who lived in dorms on campus. Their parents worked in small countries without schools, so my friends boarded during the school year and only saw their parents over the holidays. Some of them thrived in the dorms, and some did not. I knew dorm students who made poor choices like partying and even dating adult Filipino men. Others failed their classes or were frequently suspended from school. I often wondered if they did some of these things just to get their parents' attention.

Maybe you don't live in a dorm but you're hurting in a big way, and your parents don't seem to get it. If this is you, I beg you to talk with them. You have an advocate, Christ Himself, and He is mighty! Pray for wisdom, the right words, and an open heart in your mom and dad. Then talk with them honestly. I wish some of my dorm friends had told their parents, "Mom and Dad, I'm really struggling! I don't know how to process school, friends, God, and dating all by myself. I need you in my day-to-day life. Would you please consider homeschooling me or asking for a different placement so that I can live at home with you?"

Remember, just like everyone in the whole world, your parents were born with a sin nature. Anger, gossip, fear, pride—these things will always come naturally to them and to you and me! So in all your interactions with them, seek to be gracious and forgiving. Colossians 3:13 says, "Forgive as the Lord forgave you." Remember the gospel? God Almighty came down to this sinful, broken world in the form of a Man to rescue us. In physical, spiritual, and emotional *agony* He forgave us. We must do likewise.

WATCHING OUR PARENTS GET HURT IN MINISTRY

But sometimes our parents aren't the ones sinning; they're the ones being sinned against. This is also painful and confusing. When Mom and Dad are hurting, it feels like the captain of the ship has been shot. *What do we do?! Where do we turn?!*

Did you know that Moses, who had been called into leadership by God, once endured scornful criticism from his own siblings? Miriam and Aaron spoke badly about his wife because they were jealous God chose Moses as their leader. Numbers 12:1–11 tells the story. Listen to what Miriam and Aaron say in verse 2: "'Has the LORD spoken only through Moses?' they asked. 'Hasn't he also spoken through us?'" They may as well have said, "Why should we listen to this guy? Does he think he's the only one God speaks through?" Unfortunately for Aaron and Miriam, God overheard their slam-fest. In verses 4 to 15, God called Moses, Aaron, and Miriam into the tent of meeting, and God Almighty came down in a pillar of cloud. (And you thought being called into the principal's office was bad!) He fiercely rebuked Moses' brother and sister for speaking against Moses, and when the cloud lifted, Miriam was covered with leprosy. Her health was restored seven days later because Moses begged God to heal her.

But I skipped over the most incredible part of the story. Right after we learn that Miriam and Aaron were slandering Moses, verse 3 says, "Now Moses was a very humble man, more humble than anyone else on the face of the earth." Talk about high praise! He was a leader with such humility that when others tore him down, he did not defend himself. So who stepped in to defend him? *God Himself defended Moses!*

The wonderful truth is, God Almighty is the real Captain of the ship. When your parents suffer unjustly, you can trust God to defend them. When they're discouraged and directionless, you can trust God to lead them. He is always in control . . . even when the waves are crashing against the ship.

Remember, if anyone understands suffering in ministry, it's Jesus. He knows what it's like to be betrayed by friends, to be ignored when you preach the truth, to be tired and lonely. That's why you can trust Him with your parents. As much as you love them, I promise Jesus loves them more.

LIVING IN A WAR ZONE

One final reason ministry can be messy is because it takes place in a war zone. Ephesians 6:12 says, "For our struggle is not against flesh and blood, but against the rulers, against the authorities, against the powers of this dark world and against the spiritual forces of evil in the heavenly realms."

Did you know there is an invisible battle raging all around us? Ever since Satan tempted Adam and Eve to sin against God, he has been on a mission to destroy Christ-followers. The Apostle Peter likens him to a roaring lion, on the hunt for someone to devour (1 Peter 5:8). If you're like me, you may have heard these things before but failed to take them seriously. But imagine you're at the zoo, and over the intercom a voice suddenly announces that a lion is loose. All you hear is, "Hey folks, he hasn't eaten since yesterday, and we don't know where he is. So be on the lookout!" How seriously would you heed that warning? I don't know about you, but I would pole vault over the zoo gate if I had to!

Yet Peter has told me the very same thing, and so often I just casually stroll around without thinking twice about the spiritual realm around me. We've got to realize that Satan is out to destroy our faith. As people on mission to advance Christ's kingdom, we're walking around the zoo with red meat in our pockets! We are prime targets for spiritual warfare, and it's time we realized it. There is no need to fear because Jesus has already won, but there is much need to pray and exercise faith. As Paul instructs, we must put on the full armor of God: truth, righteousness, the gospel, faith, salvation, and the Word of God (Ephesians 6:13–17). We must be proactive in covering our parents, their co-laborers, and ourselves in Bible-saturated prayer. This is one of the biggest ways you can step out of the hallway and engage in Christ's mission. Lest you're feeling a little overwhelmed, let's walk together to the final truth the gospel teaches us about ministry.

OUR PERFECT PEACE IN MINISTRY

When we look at ministry through the lens of the gospel, we see it is a gift. We see it is a mess because of sin and spiritual warfare. But best of all, we see that God is in complete control! Imagine for a moment how the disciples must have felt when Jesus was crucified. Talk about a ministry disaster! Even prior to the Crucifixion, when Jesus warned them He was going to die, they couldn't accept it. Peter took Jesus aside and rebuked Him, "'Never, Lord!' he said. 'This shall never happen to you!'" (Matthew 16:22). When at last it *did* happen, the disciples went straight into crisis mode. They ran, they hid, they denied knowing Him. Sometime after Jesus' burial, we catch up with the disciples huddled together in a room with the door locked, for fear of the Jewish leaders.

Can you picture them? I wonder if they were saying, "What now? What do we do? Do you think they're going to kill all of us?" I know ministry can get rough, but I doubt many of us have been holed up in a room anticipating death! But watch what happens: "On the evening of that first day of the week, when the disciples were together, with the doors locked for fear of the Jewish leaders, Jesus came and stood among them and said, 'Peace be with you!'" (John 20:19).

Don't you just want to stand up and cheer?! There they are, shaking in their sandals, when Jesus suddenly appears, proving that all along our Triune God was in complete control! There wasn't a single second when God was going, "Oh, shoot! I didn't plan for this!" He was never in crisis mode. He was always sovereign, working through the chaos to achieve His beautiful plan—the redemption of mankind.

Beloved MK, wherever you are, God is in control. Matthew 10:29 promises that not even a sparrow falls to the ground apart from His will. He is in control of the *details* of your life! He's backstage in the chaos and confusion. He sees the pretty side of ministry, the ugly side, and the side you and I can't even see—the eternal side. If you feel overwhelmed by this life God has called you to, let His words to the disciples be His words to you today: "Peace be with you!"

It's time to let go of our anxiety. It's time to trust God with our lives, with the parts we love and the parts we hate. It's time to trust Him with our parents and their ministries. It's time to trust Him with the future, with all the questions we don't have answers to. You and I don't need all the answers. We don't need control of each and every situation. We just need to know that Jesus is still alive, and, better yet, He's right here in the room with us.

QUESTIONS FOR REFLECTION

At this point in your life, are you thankful that your family is participating in Christ's work? Why or why not?

Read Romans 3:10, 23. How do these verses explain why ministry can be messy?

After reading this chapter, is there anything you need to discuss with your parents? Write a short prayer, asking God for wisdom and humility.

As Christians, why can we have peace in the midst of difficult ministries?

Do you feel anxious about any aspect of your family's ministry? If so, read the following verses and circle one or two that stand out to you. Copy them on notecards and consider memorizing them.

> You will keep in perfect peace those whose minds are steadfast, because they trust in you. —Isaiah 26:3

> Cast your cares on the Lord and he will sustain you; he will never let the righteous be shaken. —Psalm 55:22

> Do not be anxious about anything, but in every situation, by prayer and petition, with thanksgiving, present your requests to God. And the peace of God, which transcends all understanding, will guard your hearts and your minds in Christ Jesus. —Philippians 4:6–7

The Lord is with me; I will not be afraid. What can mere mortals do to me? —Psalm 118:6

So do not fear, for I am with you; do not be dismayed, for I am your God. I will strengthen you and help you; I will uphold you with my righteous right hand. —Isaiah 41:10

CHAPTER 7

AVOIDING MK PITFALLS IN DATING

It's hard to write a book for teenagers without discussing dating. After all, adolescence is the magical time when everything starts to change between guys and girls. The boy who was once annoying becomes interesting . . . then appealing . . . then all-consuming! The girl who was once a cootie-factory becomes a fascinating mystery. But how does our MK upbringing affect our relationships with the opposite sex? To no one's surprise, being an MK uniquely impacts dating, purity, and guy-girl friendships.

WHERE IT ALL BEGAN

I was 14 years old the first time I told a boy I loved him. I really meant it too. We were a few months shy of entering high school, and I was positive I could hear wedding bells in our future. Looking back, I can pinpoint exactly what I "loved" most about him. It wasn't his looks or his personality. It wasn't his sense of humor, spirituality, or athleticism. I liked those things, but they weren't what stole my heart.

What I loved most about him was the way he made me feel about myself. He made me feel beautiful, special, and interesting. He filled a lonely ache in my heart, a secret place that always wondered, *Am I enough?* The fact that he picked me when lots of other girls liked him seemed to shout,

"Yes! You are enough!" I guess you could say I didn't really fall in love with a boy at all. I fell in love with the feeling of being wanted.

Have you ever experienced that feeling? Or perhaps *longed* to experience it? Allow me to set your mind at ease—the longing for a boyfriend or girlfriend is completely normal. In fact, our desire for companionship stretches all the way back to creation. You already know the story, but for a minute imagine being Adam, all alone with God in paradise. Can you smell the fresh garden air? There isn't a trace of sin or guilt to dampen your joy.

Yet in this perfect state, one day God looks at Adam and says, "It is not good for the man to be alone. I will make a helper suitable for him" (Genesis 2:18). So God gathers all the animals He has made and sends them to Adam, who names each one. Genesis 2:20 says, "But for Adam no suitable helper was found." In other words, it quickly becomes apparent that none of the hyenas or rhinos are quite right to be Adam's special partner. (Guys, this is where you breathe a big sigh of relief.)

In His kindness, God takes on a special project. He custom-designs a beautiful counterpart just for Adam, a creature made from Adam's own body. Adam takes one look at her and declares, "This is now bone of my bones and flesh of my flesh; she shall be called 'woman,' for she was taken out of man" (Genesis 2:23). Genesis 2:24 concludes, "That is why a man leaves his father and mother and is united to his wife, and they become one flesh."

This is an account of the very first marriage. Notice it took place before mankind had ever sinned. Adam didn't need a helper because he was broken and weak. He was in perfect relationship with God. Yet God acknowledged that it was not good for man to be alone. Clearly, having an interest in the opposite sex, or a longing to one day marry, isn't the result of sin nature. It's actually part of how God designed us.

That doesn't mean everyone is called to marriage. In 1 Corinthians 7:7 Paul praises the gift of singleness by writing, "I wish that all of you were [single] as I am. But each of you has your own gift from God; one has this gift, another has that." If you have no desire to date or one day marry, that is OK! God may give you that desire down the road, or you may have the gift of singleness. But most teenagers I know don't fall into this category. If anything, they're extremely interested in dating and one day finding a life partner. The problem is, they sometimes want to do it for the wrong reasons.

HOW IT ALL WENT WRONG

If our story ended with Adam and Eve living happily ever after in the Garden of Eden, I promise relationships would be a whole lot simpler. We would have no insecurity or anxiety. Our motives would be pure and honest. But alas, sin entered the picture and muddied our hearts.

Years after the Fall, the prophet Jeremiah declared, "The heart is deceitful above all things and beyond cure. Who can understand it?" (Jeremiah 17:9). This verse is proof that the old adage "follow your heart" just isn't wise. We cannot trust our hearts or our emotions because both are influenced by sin.

Sure, we may want to date in order to find a lifelong companion and bring glory to God. But in our brokenness, we also have impure motives. We want to date to impress others, fit in, satisfy our hormones, boost our egos, and quench our loneliness. The good and the bad are all jumbled up together. So let's sort it out, shall we? Let's look at four of the most common relationship pitfalls MKs slip into, and let's see how the Bible can train us.

TOO MUCH TOO SOON

In her book *Belonging Everywhere and Nowhere*, therapist Lois Bushong suggests that third culture kids are known for developing deep relationships quickly. I've known this for years. Actually, it's one of my favorite things about TCKs! We tend to skip all the chitchat and dive straight into meaningful relationships. Bushong elaborates by referencing Professor John Powell, who created a chart of five different levels of communication. The most superficial level is the fifth level, which Powell called "cliché conversation." This is basically small talk in which people exchange polite pleasantries without really saying anything. The fourth level is called "reporting the facts." At this stage, people still don't talk about themselves. They're just sharing news. In level three, "my ideas and judgments," people begin to share personal opinions, thoughts, or decisions. Powell called level two "my feelings," and this is gut-level sharing. Conversations become more vulnerable as people reveal who they are and how they feel. Finally, level one is "peak communication." At this point, there is total openness and honesty.

In American culture, conversations typically begin at level five, and slowly progress deeper, depending on the relationship. But Bushong writes, "For whatever reason, one characteristic of TCKs is that many of them jump directly into level three." We start sharing snippets of our thoughts, ideas, and ultimately *ourselves* almost immediately. Why? Some people think it's because we move a lot. In other words, there's no time to waste. We've got to make friends, and do it posthaste! Others believe TCKs are more willing to be vulnerable because our nomadic lifestyle gives us a false sense of security. It's less threatening to open up to others when we assume we'll be leaving in a few months anyway. A third theory is that different cultures simply approach conversation differently.

Regardless of the rationale behind it, diving into a deep relationship quickly has its pros and cons. While MKs are good at forging meaningful connections, we open ourselves up to a lot of potential heartache. For one thing, our friendliness can be misunderstood. As a teenager on furlough in America, one of the first cultural cues I picked up on was that people don't make eye contact with strangers. In the Philippines it is customary to look everyone in the eye and smile whether you know them or not. But I quickly learned that American boys get the wrong idea if you look at them and smile for no reason!

The same thing can happen if we converse freely and openly in a culture that's used to more guarded conversation. People of the same sex may perceive our frank dialogue as invasive. People of the opposite sex may get the impression that we want a deeper, more serious relationship with them. If we don't catch the social cues and back off, the results can be awkward at best and compromising at worst.

A friend of mine once told me about just such a situation. One night, while on furlough in the States, she went bowling with some friends. At the bowling alley, a group of American boys approached her and struck up a conversation. Most American teens realize that if a peer of the opposite sex randomly initiates conversation with you, he or she is probably romantically interested in you. But to my friend who had grown up overseas, it was common to talk freely with strangers. So she was her usual self—warm, open, and engaging. The boys immediately misread her friendliness as flirtation, and before long they had turned the conversation in an embarrassing direction. By the time they were making inappropriate references to her curvy figure and inviting her to go out with them, she knew something wasn't right. Thankfully, she had girlfriends around to help her get out of that situation. But it could have been compromising and even dangerous had she been alone.

But what if you actually *want* a deeper relationship with someone? Why is it harmful to dive into a serious relationship if you really *like* the other person? To answer that question, let's take a look at Proverbs 4. This beautiful proverb is written from the perspective of a father speaking to his son about wise living. After giving his son 22 verses worth of advice, the father finally says, "*Above all else*, guard your heart, for everything you do flows from it" (Proverbs 4:23, author's emphasis).

Above all else. It's like the father was saying, "Listen son, *more than anything else*, guard your heart! That's the most important thing, and it will affect everything else in your life." Jumping into an emotionally deep dating relationship is like swinging the doors of your heart wide open. It's like announcing, "Come on in! Know all of me! I'm going to give you my love, my vulnerability, my secrets, my whole heart." Hollywood says this is romantic. The Bible says it's foolish.

Remember that 14-year-old boy I thought I'd marry one day? Not long after I told him I loved him, he lost interest in me. Soon he was dating someone else. You want to hear something crazy? Even as an adult who's happily married with four children, in difficult seasons I sometimes dream I'm back in high school and that same boy is rejecting me all over again. It happened decades ago! But it impacted me deeply. The more I offered this boy my heart, the more I stitched my identity to him. When he "loved" me, I believed I was lovely, and when he lost interest, I believed I was inadequate. Without even meaning to, I had allowed a human's opinion to become more valuable to me than God's opinion, and the result was emotionally disastrous.

The scars run even deeper when we become physically involved with a boyfriend or girlfriend. And trust me, emotional intimacy eventually leads to physical intimacy. Again, this is part of our design. Within the safe covenant of marriage, emotional and physical intimacy are beautiful gifts. But outside of marriage, they are recipes for heartbreak. Precious MK, "Above all else, guard your heart, for everything you do flows from it" (Proverbs 4:23).

How do we guard our hearts practically? The same way we would guard a city—we set up borders, or boundaries, for protection. Here are some examples of boundaries with the opposite sex:

- I will not date until I'm old enough to marry. Until then, I will cultivate friendships with the opposite sex.
- I will only date someone who is a true follower of Jesus.
- I will not be alone in a room or a car with a member of the opposite sex.
- I will not share vulnerable details with someone until I am engaged or seriously considering engagement.

These are just a few examples of boundaries that help safeguard our hearts. Remember, a truly effective boundary is one that's set along the far perimeter of your heart. Back in biblical times when they used walls to protect their cities, where do you think they built the walls? Right around the king's home? Of course not! They built them along the perimeter of the city. That way if an enemy broke through, he would still have a long way to go before he could destroy what was most precious to them. When we set boundaries like, "I will do anything with my boyfriend or girlfriend except have sex," we're attempting to protect a city by building a wall right around the king's castle. It's foolish, and we're likely to end up wounded.

THE LONELINESS TRAP

Another way to safeguard our hearts is to recognize where they're weak. Moving around a lot as an MK leaves pockets of loneliness in our hearts. If we don't learn to find comfort in Christ, we become vulnerable to dating for the wrong reasons. Much of why I pined for a boyfriend in high school was because I felt so lonely living halfway across the world from my friends. I wanted a companion to satisfy that ache. But remember, Eve was designed to be Adam's helper . . . not his God. The deepest aches of our hearts will only ever be satisfied in God alone. That's why the psalmist once wrote, "As the deer pants for streams of water, so my soul pants for you, my God. My soul thirsts for God, for the living God. When can I go and meet with God?" (Psalm 42:1–2).

Throughout the Bible we see the metaphor of God being "living water" and our hearts "thirsting" for Him. Do you remember the story of Jesus' encounter with the Samaritan woman at the well? She had been married to five different men, and was at that time involved with a sixth man who was not her husband. Had she gone to a public high school, she was the kind of girl who would've been called a lot of choice names. But doesn't it sound like she was just trying to fill the loneliness in her heart with relationship . . . after relationship . . . after relationship? In that sense, she's not that different than we are. We know Jesus is supposed to satisfy us, but deep down we long for "Mr. or Ms. Perfect" because we believe the right relationship will fill all the empty corners of our hearts.

But Jesus looks at this broken woman and says, "If you knew the gift of God and who it is that asks you for a drink, you would have asked him and he would have given you living water" (John 4:10). Jesus goes on to promise, "Everyone who drinks this water [from this well] will be thirsty again, but whoever drinks the water I give them will never thirst. Indeed, the water I give them will become in them a spring of water welling up to eternal life" (John 4:13–14).

You can marry the most awesome person you've ever met (like I did!), and you will thirst again. The godliest guy or girl on the planet cannot be living water for you. Listen to these haunting words from Jeremiah 2:13: "My people have committed two sins: they have forsaken me, the spring of living water, and have dug their own cisterns, broken cisterns that cannot hold water." Don't believe the lie that the right person can quench your loneliness. The coolest guy or the sweetest girl on campus is still a broken cistern. They were never designed to hold living water.

Only when our hearts are satisfied in Christ are they truly ready to be offered to others. When we are content and nourished in Jesus, we don't develop needy, clingy relationships. Instead, we're free to love and care for others in a healthy, God-honoring way.

THE ONLINE ESCAPE

A third pitfall for MKs that is closely linked to the loneliness trap is the online escape. Sometimes we don't run to a relationship to fill our loneliness. Instead we look to a screen for comfort. Whether it's a television, computer, tablet, or phone screen, all these have one thing in common—they're not rooted in reality. They serve as a temporary escape from the real world.

Different people like to escape to different places in the virtual world. Some people spend hours on social media. Understandably, social media is appealing to MKs because it's a means of connecting the dots between all our different worlds. We can keep up with friends in Zimbabwe, Prague, Malaysia . . . you name it! But though we may feel socially connected while we're peering into other people's online lives, the minute we power off, we often feel lonelier than ever.

It's just as easy to escape to online shopping, gaming, or digital streaming sites where we numb ourselves for hours. More dangerously, we can slip into darker corners, such as chat rooms and pornography sites, which threaten our safety and our souls. In his book *Wired for Intimacy*, William Struthers uses the example of hikers on a path to explain the damaging effects of pornography. If hikers travel on the same path over and over again, it will eventually grow wider and deeper. Similarly, repeated exposure to porn creates pathways in the brain. The more someone views porn, the more his or her brain associates the opposite sex with pornographic images. Struthers writes, "[People who view porn] have unknowingly created a neurological circuit that imprisons their ability to see women [and men] rightly as created in God's image." These neural pathways are part of why pornography is so addictive and enslaving. Author Heath Lambert writes, "I know dozens of people (men and women) who struggle with pornography . . . At the beginning of the journey [it] seemed fun, intriguing, comforting, and exhilarating. Now, the sin has bitten back hard. Their hearts are weighed down with guilt, their relationships are strained, their view of sex is corrupted, and their Christian witness is marred."

Why do we venture into these sinful places? One answer may be as simple as this: in the real world, it's hard to fit in. There are seasons in an MK's life when the feeling of being an outsider is especially intense. During those seasons, it's easier to hide behind a screen than it is to form real-life relationships. When you're unhappy with the country you've been forced to live in, it's more appealing to maintain virtual friendships than to make new ones. In this way, the screen becomes the ultimate hallway to hide in. You're on the outside looking in, and no one can see you hiding there. The problem is that the online escape is bitterly deceptive. It is a world of contradictions. It feels emotionally safe, but it's actually incredibly dangerous. It offers social connections, but in reality it leaves us isolated and alone. It disguises itself as a path to limitless freedom while being highly addictive and enslaving. We run to it for fulfillment, but it leaves us emptier than ever.

To see whether or not you've fallen prey to the online escape, ask yourself these questions:

- Do I spend more than two hours every day indulging in some form of screen time?
- Is screen time my only form of recreation, or do I have other hobbies?
- Do my parents know and approve of the amount of time I spend online?
- Can I honestly say there is not even a hint of sexual immorality in my online life? (Ephesians 5:3)
- Would I panic if I couldn't access my phone for a day?
- Have I ever tried to stop or reduce my screen time and found myself unable to do it?
- When I feel upset, lonely, or bored, do I turn to my phone or computer?

One of the most powerful ways the gospel speaks to the online escape is through the incarnation of Christ. Don't let that fancy word throw you! The word *incarnation* simply refers to the act of God coming to earth as a man. John 1:14 describes it like this, "The Word (Jesus) became flesh and made his dwelling among us. We have seen his glory, the glory of the one and only Son, who came from the Father, full of grace and truth."

Why is this so significant? Because God Almighty literally put on human skin in order to come to earth and *know* us. He didn't set up an online profile and invite us to "follow" Him or "friend" Him. He came as a flesh-and-blood Person, to have a real relationship with us. For 33 years, He walked on the same dirt of planet earth that we walk on. He was tempted just like we are (but He never gave in to temptation). He understands our weaknesses (Hebrews 4:15). Jesus never wanted a phony, superficial relationship with us; He came with the intent for intimacy. After He ascended into heaven, He sent the Holy Spirit to continue an intimate relationship with us, and the Bible promises that Christ Himself dwells within all true believers (Colossians 1:27; John 15:4).

Beloved child of God, you don't have to hide behind a screen to soothe the aches of your heart with fake relationships, mind-numbing entertainment, or images that make you feel shameful and worthless. Jesus offers you a real relationship with Him, and He alone can enable you to forge real, meaningful relationships with others.

TEMPTATION ISLAND

There's one final pitfall we need to examine before moving on. Unlike the others, this pitfall isn't necessarily the result of inward turmoil like loneliness or insecurity. For MKs it's more often the result of innocence or naïveté, like a big pothole in the middle of the road that catches us unaware. I like to think of it as Temptation Island.

In 2001, Fox premiered a reality show with that very title: *Temptation Island*. I was 17 years old and forbidden to watch it. I did, however, catch enough of the advertisements to know the show was built on a scandalous premise. Couples traveled to a remote island where their relationships were put to the test. The men were separated from their girlfriends and surrounded by scantily clad supermodels. The women, likewise, were surrounded by gorgeous men, who (at least in the commercials) seemed to spend a lot of time bare-chested. The point of the show was to see whether or not the couples would stay true to one another.

I've often thought that returning to your parents' home country is a lot like taking a trip to Temptation Island. People who work with MKs have a term for the feelings we face when transitioning off the mission field. They call it "reentry shock." One of the first shocking things I noticed as a 15-year-old returning to the US was the amount of skin girls showed in my public high school. I had never seen shorts and skirts so short in my life! But that was just the beginning. I gawked at students who kissed in the hallways, cringed at the language I heard, and kept an ongoing mental list of questionable topics to decipher. I felt as if I needed an urban dictionary to understand the things my fellow classmates were casually discussing. Then one day, I made a new friend who discovered how little I actually understood and happily obliged to fill me in on everything. I mean everything. I went home, burst into my mom's room, and blurted, "You would not *believe* what kids are doing these days!"

Why is reentry into our home country so shocking? Typically, MKs grow up in sheltered environments. We're raised in Christian homes and are often surrounded by Christian communities such as churches, mission organizations, MK schools, and the like. Sometimes technology is remote. There may be a handful of fuzzy TV channels or enough Internet buffering to make online streaming pointless. In a lot of cultures, there's a higher standard of modesty as well. Add all of these factors together, and you begin to understand why we may be in for a shock when we transition off the mission field. The opportunities to sin seem boundless. Temptation is even more intense if we make the transition around the time we're entering college and living apart from our parents.

Now obviously, there are exceptions. Some MKs grow up in extremely immodest cultures or have access to highly advanced technology. A lot depends on your parents' ministry location. But if you're an MK from a more sheltered background, Temptation Island may be a real threat for you. How do you prepare?

Before transitioning off the mission field, recognize your sin tendencies. We all have different weaknesses, so get real about the areas where you struggle. Talk with your parents about these areas so they can pray for you, protect you, and provide accountability. James 5:16 says, "Therefore confess your sins to each other and pray for each other so that you may be healed." If you're struggling with pornography or sexual sin, it is brave and obedient (not shameful) to tell your parents about that struggle. There are resources listed at the end of this chapter that you can study together with your parents (or a trusted, godly adult, such as a small group leader or pastor), which can help you walk toward freedom. Furthermore, your parents can take practical measures to limit your access to technology as you transition off the mission field. They are God's gift of protection to you. Don't leave them in the dark.

Perhaps you don't wrestle with sexual sin, but you struggle with body image and the desire to fit in. Recognize that modesty will be especially challenging when you transition off the mission field. Temptation Island is a world where fashion, conformity, and materialism are highly emphasized. Again, enlist your parents for godly accountability. Girls, begin memorizing Bible verses such as 1 Peter 3:3–4 and Proverbs 31:30 to combat the lies Temptation Island likes to tell. Guys, perhaps Job 31:1 and 1 Timothy 4:12 would be helpful to memorize. At the end of the day, as we navigate adolescence, purity, and guy-girl relationships, it all comes back to guarding our hearts.

A CITY UNDER ATTACK

We must guard our hearts with the same passion and vigilance with which we would guard a city that's under attack. Because we *are* under attack (Ephesians 6:12). But thankfully we are not defenseless. We have the weapons of community, prayer, God's Word, and the gospel of Jesus Christ.

Yes, mankind messed up God's beautiful gifts of gender, marriage, sex, and companionship, but Jesus redeemed all of it when He went to the Cross! No matter how many mistakes you've made in the area of purity, it is not too late to repent and be restored by Christ. The Book of Isaiah talks about how God's people continually rebelled against Him. They were so stubborn, always wanting to do things their own way. But in Isaiah 30:18, the prophet Isaiah declares, "Yet the LORD longs to be gracious to you; therefore he will rise up to show you compassion." In the next verse Isaiah goes on to say, "How gracious he will be when you cry for help! As soon as he hears, he will answer you" (Isaiah 30:19). This is the heart of God—strong and steadfast, merciful and compassionate. Won't you throw away those broken cisterns? Come to Him and be restored. Drink of Him and be satisfied.

QUESTIONS FOR REFLECTION

Have you ever felt embarrassed about wanting a boyfriend/girlfriend or about being attracted to the opposite sex? Based on Genesis 2, why is it normal (and even good) to have an interest in the opposite sex? How did it all go wrong?

What are some of the dangers of rushing into a dating relationship? Have you ever regretted sharing too much of your heart with a member of the opposite sex? If so, what could you do differently in the future?

Reread Jeremiah 2:13. Why do you think we're tempted to look for fulfillment from human relationships instead of from God? Why is it foolish to expect a person to satisfy the deepest desires of our hearts?

Reread the questions from "the online escape" section. Based on your answers to these questions, what needs to change in your life?

Do you think you've had a sheltered upbringing? Why or why not?

Of the four pitfalls discussed in this chapter, which one do you struggle with the most? Are there any other pitfalls you would add to this list?

RECOMMENDED (NON-GRAPHIC) RESOURCES:

Finally Free: Fighting for Purity with the Power of Grace by Heath Lambert— This book is specifically geared toward those battling pornography.

Purity is Possible: How to Live Free of the Fantasy Trap by Helen Thorne— This book is written for females struggling with lust and/or pornography.

Sex Is Not the Problem (Lust Is): Sexual Purity in a Lust-Saturated World by Joshua Harris—This book is for guys or girls struggling with lust personally and in dating relationships.

Boundaries in Dating: How Healthy Choices Grow Healthy Relationships by Henry Cloud and John Townsend—This book will help you set healthy, biblical parameters for dating relationships.

CHAPTER 8

WHY CROSS-CULTURAL PRIDE IS COSTLY

Everyone knows the story. It's one of Aesop's famous fables. Once upon a time a tortoise and a hare set off to race, with laughably unequal odds. (Picture Grandma challenging The Flash to a quick lap around the block!) Eventually, our furry Flash decides he is so far ahead, he may as well take a nap in the middle of the race. Why not? He passed the tortoise miles ago! But when the hare wakes up, he discovers he has lost the race to his slow and steady opponent.

Growing up if you asked me which character I felt like, I would've picked the tortoise: quiet, unsure of myself, and known to run a 20-minute mile. With my inhaler. (Horrible asthma, don't ask!) But *spiritually* speaking, I have always been the hare. The odds have been stacked in my favor. I was born into a Christian family who wholeheartedly loved Jesus. My parents taught me Bible stories from the time I could hold my head upright . . . never mind there was drool running down my face! Seeing Mom counsel a weeping woman in the living room was as commonplace as brushing my teeth before bed. Sound familiar? In many ways, MKs have every spiritual advantage. The problem is, like the hare, we lose sight of the race set before us.

RUNNING THE RACE

Did you know you're running in a race right this very minute? Obviously it's not a physical race but a spiritual one. Hebrews 12:1 says, "Let us throw off everything that hinders and the sin that so easily entangles. And let us *run with perseverance the race marked out for us*" (author's emphasis). What is this race? Simply put, it's the Christian life. It's our journey from the moment we surrender our hearts to Jesus until we cross the finish line and land in His arms.

Isn't it interesting that of all the images God could've used to describe the Christian life, He likens it to a race? When I think of a race, I think of words like *endurance, training, sacrifice,* and *passion*. The scary thing is, when I think of my own life, those same words don't exactly spring to mind. Instead, words like *distractions, anxiety,* and *exhaustion* come to mind. Maybe when you consider your life, you think of words like *popularity, pressure,* and *approval*. Or *boredom, anger,* and *indifference*. But here's the sobering reality: whether we're running like a champion or fast asleep under a tree, you and I are *in* the race.

The Apostle Paul understood this. He realized there is a purpose for life on earth, and he could either ignore it, half-heartedly pursue it, or chase it with the dedication of an Olympian. He chose the latter. In 1 Corinthians 9:19–23, Paul ardently declares that he is willing to do whatever it takes to win people to Jesus. Now listen closely to his next words:

> Do you not know that in a race all the runners run, but only one gets the prize? Run in such a way as to get the prize. Everyone who competes in the games goes into strict training. They do it to get a crown that will not last, but we do it to get a crown that will last forever. Therefore I do not run like someone running aimlessly; I do not fight like a boxer beating the air. No, I strike a blow to my body and make it my slave so that after I have preached to others, I myself will not be disqualified for the prize. —1 Corinthians 9:24–27

Sometimes athletes quote this passage out of context to inspire themselves to get in shape. But Paul himself acknowledged that in an earthly race the crown does not last. Remember, the race Paul is describing is spiritual. It's the steady, faithful life of a true Christian who keeps on going . . . and going . . . and going. Just like the tortoise. Unlike earthly competitions, the purpose of this race is not to polish your ego or compete with other Christians. The purpose is to know Christ until, like Paul, you come to believe Jesus is so worthy of worship you're willing to do whatever it takes to make Him famous in our world.

SNORING ON THE SIDELINES

But it's hard to live this way, isn't it? How many MKs do you know who are basically snoring under a tree somewhere? They're bored at church. They don't really care about sharing their faith. They're just going through the motions. Perhaps that's you. If so, I can relate. There was a season in my MK journey when I completely lost sight of the race. I didn't lose my salvation or renounce Jesus, I just sort of . . . fell asleep. I became apathetic about knowing and obeying Christ.

Sometimes this sort of apathy creeps into our lives simply because we're human and sinful. But sometimes it sneaks in for uniquely MK reasons. Like the hare, we can develop false confidence. After all, Dad and Mom are "pro athletes" when it comes to running the spiritual race. They're running hard enough for everybody, right? *(Hey, pass me the ice cream while we chill in the hallway, would you?)* Hopefully by now you understand why that thinking is wrong. But there's another reason we can lose sight of the race. Sometimes our MK pride and heartache blind us to it. Let me give you an example.

If there's one thing MKs have in abundance, it's cool stories. Surprisingly, for me this was one of the toughest things about moving back to America. The more I got to know my new classmates, the more I felt like they had barely lived. *You've never been outside of Florida? Your wildest adventures revolve around boys and the mall? Seriously?*

Granted, I never voiced any of these thoughts, but I began to feel superior to these small-minded peers of mine. All I wanted to do was tell stories that put their pathetic lives to shame. After all, I was a treasure trove of amazing experiences! I had visited remote Filipino tribes. I had ducked on the school bus (more than once) when men with rifles pulled us over. I had slept in the open air on exotic beaches and helped kill, pluck, gut, and (almost) eat a chicken in a village! I breathed French air from the top of the Eiffel Tower, and I held orphans in my arms in Africa . . . and now I was listening to a story about prank calls at a sleepover? *Awesome.*

On one particularly agonizing afternoon shortly after I arrived in the US, my parents introduced me to a co-worker's daughter. Hoping to make a friend, since I had exactly zero to my name, I listened politely as she pulled out a photo album and told me all about her recent mission trip to who knows where. I still can't remember. What I do remember were the 800 photographs she showed me. One at a time. With each photograph she included a detailed description about the things they ate, smelled, saw, *blah, blah, blah* . . . I wanted to cry. I missed the Philippines so badly I could barely breathe, and she never asked me a single question about my life there. For two hours she told me about her three weeks in a foreign country, and each of the 15 years I had lived overseas burned in my chest.

Bit by bit, my heartache morphed into disdain. Have you ever had similar feelings? Have you felt superior to kids who've never traveled? Or kids who only speak one language? Have you laughed at kids who ask questions like, *"So is Asia a city or a country?"* Have you made fun of them with other MKs? I have. You want to hear an honest confession? It felt good. I was so used to being an outsider that it felt great to be on the inside of a joke every now and then. It felt great to get with other MKs and laugh at everyone else, instead of being the one everyone else was laughing at.

But God never intended for our experiences to make us arrogant. He didn't expose us to poverty and culture and world religions so that we would look down our noses at the small-town girl who's never flown on an airplane. As a matter of fact, God has an opposite plan. He gave us these experiences to make us more like Jesus, who loves the *whole world*. Guess what? That includes the kids who've never flown on airplanes. Jesus has a heart for them, and that means we should too.

James 4:6 tells us, "God opposes the proud but shows favor to the humble." As MKs, we must stand guard against pride. We must be so thankful for the special things God has allowed us to see and experience. We must recognize that exposure to the world is a gift. But we must remind ourselves that if it makes us arrogant, it's worthless.

Worse yet, it's dangerous. In my case, pride had me snoozing on the sidelines, completely indifferent to the spiritual race around me. I had little interest in loving my new classmates or sharing the gospel with them because I was too busy nursing my heartache and silently sneering. Thankfully, in His great grace, God finally shook me awake. He did it in the most unexpected way—through the death of the founder of our organization, Dr. Bill Bright.

———

It was the summer of 2003, and I had just graduated from high school. Every other year we had a massive staff conference in Colorado, and this year, with the death of Bill Bright, things were especially sober. One night there was a memorial service to honor him. I sat in a stadium with thousands of other staff families and watched a video about Dr. Bright's life. I learned that he was known to put his head on his desk and weep when he thought about lost people. I learned that despite ministering to thousands of people globally, every few years he invited one man into his life to mentor personally. I learned that as a young man, he wrote and signed a contract surrendering his life to Christ's kingdom work. And I learned that as he died a painful death, his greatest prayer request was that he would honor God in the midst of his suffering.

After the memorial service, I found a quiet spot outside, sank to my knees, and burst into tears. You know how people talk about their lives flashing before their eyes? I felt like I saw missed opportunities flashing before mine. I saw all the chances God had given me to impact the students in my public high school. I thought of all their suffering—their broken homes and broken hearts. I could not believe that in my pride and pain, I had forgotten the race. Eternity hung in the balance, and I was asleep on the sidelines.

If pieces of my story resonate with you, it's possible God is in the process of gently waking you up also. We've talked about why MKs tend to fall asleep in the middle of the race, but how do we wake up? How do we faithfully and passionately follow Jesus through all the ups and downs of life? Do we memorize more Bible verses? Hand out gospel tracts at the mall? Agree to become a missionary like Mom and Dad? Any one of those things may be the *result* of becoming serious about the race we're running, but none of those things is the *means* for running the race. Pay attention now because this is the best part! Right after the author of Hebrews urges us to run the race with perseverance, he tells us exactly how to do it: "Let us run with endurance the race that is set before us, *fixing our eyes on Jesus*, the author and perfecter of faith, who for the joy set before Him endured the cross, despising the shame, and has sat down at the right hand of the throne of God" (Hebrews 12:1–2 NASB, author's emphasis).

Pause for a second and reread those five italicized words: *fixing our eyes on Jesus.* That's the answer! How do we live out our faith? Or love people we don't feel like loving? By looking to Jesus! How do we honor our parents when they make us mad? Or trust God when we don't understand Him? We look to Jesus. We fix our eyes on who Jesus is and what He has done.

WHO JESUS IS

Jesus is the author of our faith. In other words, any faith we have comes from Him, not us. This is great news! Have you ever felt like it was hard to believe in Jesus because you couldn't see Him? My kids tell me this all the time. You know what I tell them? "It's OK that you find it difficult to believe in Jesus. *Jesus* is big enough to help you believe in Him! Ask Him to help you."

We must understand that Jesus is the author of our faith! We can't muster it up by ourselves. If you're struggling to believe God, ask Him to give you the faith to believe Him. Faith in God *comes* from God.

Jesus is also the perfecter of our faith, which means He alone *grows* it. I had a professor in Bible college who used to say, "God is not in a hurry. He grows things." He said it over and over again, and 13 years later it still comforts me. Precious MK, you don't have to have it all together. You don't have to try and be a super-Christian all by yourself. God is not in a hurry. He's growing you day by day. And He is *very good* at growing things! As a matter of fact, that's one of His specialties.

WHAT JESUS HAS DONE

But we don't just fix our eyes on who Jesus is. We also fix our eyes on what He has done. Look at the text another time: "Let us run with endurance the race that is set before us, fixing our eyes on Jesus, the author and perfecter of faith, *who for the joy set before Him endured the cross, despising the shame, and has sat down at the right hand of the throne of God*" (Hebrews 12:1–2 NASB, author's emphasis).

What did Jesus do for us? He endured the shameful Cross for the joy of saving mankind! Jesus embraced ultimate suffering for the joy of proving once and for all that God is both just and merciful. Best of all, Jesus won! He didn't just die on the Cross, He defeated death. Notice that the passage says Jesus "sat down at the right hand of the throne of God." Did you know that the priests who used to offer sacrifices for the people never sat down? They constantly stood because their work was never finished. This is so cool, you have to read it for yourself!

Day after day every priest stands and performs his religious duties; again and again he offers the same sacrifices, which can never take away sins. But when this priest [Jesus] had offered for all time one sacrifice for sins, he sat down at the right hand of God. . . . For by one sacrifice he has made perfect forever those who are being made holy. —Hebrews 10:11–12, 14

With one sacrifice—the sacrifice of His own life—Jesus rescued us forever! He was the only priest who could finally sit down because He alone *finished* the work. This is the gospel! And it is the key to our entire Christian lives. How do we live faithfully? By looking to the gospel. You see, our hearts are never revived by spiritual to-do lists and guilty promises to try harder. Our hearts are revived by the gospel. The gospel is like the folks at the cold water stand in the middle of the race who cheer aloud, *"Do not grow weary! Do not lose heart! See who your Savior is. See what your Savior has done."*

THE EVIL TWIN

In chapter 1, I challenged you to consider the fact that you may be believing a false gospel. I compared false gospels to an evil twin who parades around in disguise, damaging our view of the real gospel. Here's one way to see through the evil twin's disguise: false gospels always urge us to fix our eyes on *ourselves*.

When I was in seventh grade, I won the girls' Christian character award in school. I will never forget that award because it simultaneously filled me with pride and crushed me with shame. On one hand, it felt awesome strutting on stage to receive my public pat on the back. But no sooner had I returned to my seat than doubt crept in. *"If only they knew the rumor I started about Jennifer because I envy her. If only they knew I made fun of Leah's shoes last week. If only they knew all the awful things I think and say and do . . ."*

I felt like a prize-winning apple with a worm on the inside. And as different girls in my class eyed the certificate in my hand, I feared they were thinking exactly what I was: *"You don't deserve that."* This was how I weighed my Christian walk all through middle and high school:

- "I did my devotions every day this week. I am an *awesome* Christian!"
- "I yelled at my parents. I am a *terrible* Christian."

- "I was *so* nice to Jennifer. I definitely deserved that Christian character award!"
- "My gossiping is out of control—am I even saved?"

Just to make life more unbearable, I would often throw non-spiritual things like grades and sports into the evaluation. Eventually, my mom would find me sobbing in bed, "Everything in my life is just falling apart! Studying, reading the Bible, student government, volleyball, cheerleading . . . and have you even seen how messy my room is? I can't handle it!"

Somewhere along the way I had come to believe that my standing with God had everything to do with my performance, not with Christ's performance on my behalf. In my case, this false gospel had me racing on a treadmill and getting nowhere fast. I was exhausted, frustrated, and constantly on the brink of an emotional meltdown.

In others the same false gospel produces the opposite effect. They just quit trying. They grow embittered by a God they can never please and resolve to please themselves instead. They think about what they want to do, what feels good to them, why they deserve this or that. Either way the evil twin has convinced us both to fix our eyes on ourselves.

But an understanding of the true gospel will always point us back to Jesus. The evil twin urges us to think of what we do, how we fail, and how we might better ourselves. But the True Son tells us to think of what He has done, how He has succeeded, and how He alone has the power to forgive and transform us. Only by looking to Him can we cross the finish line.

RETRO NIGHT GLOW

So which one are you? Are you the hare, the person with every spiritual advantage who's snoring on the sidelines? Or are you the tortoise, faithfully running the race one step at a time with your eyes fixed on the prize?

I recently volunteered at a local race for charity called Retro Night Glow. Prior to the race, I heard rumors that the course was really difficult.

But when the runners took off, I learned something special about Retro Night Glow. Every single mile was marked with something cool—cheering people covered in glow sticks, a rock band playing in the middle of the road, water stations with people dressed up in costumes, a tunnel covered with inspirational quotes. It was enough to make me wish I had signed up to run the race instead of just volunteer on the sidelines!

To me, the Christian life is a little bit like Retro Night Glow. The course is difficult, and there are bound to be times when you feel like giving up. But along the way, there are all these amazing things God wants us to see, do, and experience. In fact, I believe that as MKs the opportunities are especially unique and incredible. We're about to discuss those opportunities in the next two chapters. But before we do, let's ask God to wake us up. The race is already underway. It's time to strap on some glow sticks and start running!

QUESTIONS FOR REFLECTION

What are some of the "spiritual advantages" you have as an MK?

What are some of the things that distract you from living for Christ?

Have you ever felt superior to non-MKs because of your experiences?

How might this pride damage your witness?

Read Proverbs 18:12 and 29:23. According to these two verses, what is the consequence of pride? What is the reward for humility (or a "lowly spirit")?

Read Hebrews 12:2–3. What is the secret for running the race effectively?

At this point in your life, would you describe yourself as someone who is actively living for Christ or someone who is asleep on the sidelines? Explain your answer.

CHAPTER 9

BECOMING MISSIONAL IN YOUR HOST CULTURE

In 1997 Starbucks arrived in the Philippines. Before long a massive, two-story franchise opened up just a few blocks from my house. To my 13-year-old eyes, it looked vaguely like paradise!

One morning, my dad took me on a date to Starbucks. We got our drinks and headed upstairs to my favorite spot. As I guzzled my Frappuccino, I happened to glance out the window. There, digging through a garbage can, were two street children about my age.

Do you want to know the really shocking thing? For a moment, it didn't even faze me. I grew up in a world where impoverished people slept under every bridge in the city, and dirty little hands knocked on our car windows at every red light. In fact, my dad told me when we traveled back to the United States for the first time that I asked him where all the street children were. I couldn't imagine a world without them.

But that day, as I watched those boys digging through garbage, I started to feel queasy. It was like I had stepped into one of those little activity books with a "What's Wrong with This Picture?" page. *Everything,* I thought. *Everything is wrong with this picture.* How could I slurp an expensive treat through a straw while two little boys just ten feet away from me were starving?

EYES WIDE OPEN

If you, like me, are an MK who has been guilty of falling asleep in the midst of the race, I have incredible news for you. When you finally wake up and look around, it's likely you will realize that you are in the *prime position* to impact the world for Christ. Chances are you live in a culture where the spiritual and physical needs of those around you are profound. You may live in a closed country, where the majority of people are hostile to the gospel. You may live in an unreached country, where nobody has ever heard the gospel. You may live in a third world country, where poverty is rampant. You may live in an agnostic culture, where there is a deep disregard for God. Or a pantheistic culture, where people search for hope by worshipping nature. I could go on and on.

Yes, every place on planet Earth desperately needs the gospel. But some places are much harder to reach than others. Before even venturing into open countries with religious freedoms, missionaries must undergo significant training to overcome language and cultural barriers to sharing the gospel. They must learn what the people are like socially, spiritually, and intellectually. They must learn local customs and values; otherwise, they run the risk of offending people and closing instead of opening doors to the gospel.

This kind of understanding can take years to glean. But not for you! If you've lived in your host country for most of your life, or even a handful of years, you already understand the culture and the people. Better yet, you've gained this understanding the most authentic way possible, not through a book or training session but through *living* among the people! Through watching their festivals, eating their food, bartering in their markets, walking their streets.

I'll never forget stopping by my local bank in Georgia one November in 2013. It was a busy morning, and I was in a hurry, but the minute I walked through the glass doors, I froze. There, on multiple television screens, I saw live footage of Typhoon Haiyan ravaging the Philippines. Filipino men, women, and children were screaming and floating in what looked like an ocean, clinging to random, drifting objects. I had not visited the Philippines for over a decade, but I could have dropped to my knees in horror. These weren't just people in a foreign country. These were *my* people . . . from *my* country! I may not be Filipino, but I spent 15 years of my life making that country my home. To this day, I can pick out a Filipino accent in a crowd. I can spot Filipinos just by looking at them. I know the smell and taste of their food, and the sounds of the city in the middle of rush hour. Although the country is open and considered reached, I know it is extremely poor and that the people are staunchly Roman Catholic. I know that the vast majority believe they must earn salvation and that some even physically abuse themselves in hopes of gaining favor with God.

In so many ways, I was the perfect person to share the gospel with Filipinos. I just had to wake up to all the needs around me. What about you? Are you beginning to see why God never called MKs to "hallway living"? To the life of a spectator? We have so much more potential than that! And He has a plan for us *right where we are.*

JESUS, THE MK

Do you remember how we talked about Jesus leaving His home in heaven to come to a place where He would never fully belong? There's a sense in which we could view Jesus as the very first MK. His Father had a mission to save the world, and Jesus allowed Himself to be uprooted because of it. But imagine if that's *all* Jesus agreed to do. Imagine if He told the Father, "Fine! I'll go because You're making me go, but don't expect me to be happy about it. I'm giving You the bare minimum, and that's it!"

Yet isn't that what we're sometimes tempted to do? When the going gets tough, it's easy to cross our arms and snap, "Fine! I'll switch schools again, but don't expect me to get excited about your work! I'll do what you make me do, and not one thing more."

But Jesus adopted the opposite attitude. In the face of extreme sacrifice, He wholeheartedly embraced the Father's mission *as His own.* He devoted His life to the mission. Read the following passage and see if you can spot both Jesus' outward *actions* and His inward heart *attitude:*

Jesus went through all the towns and villages, teaching in their synagogues, proclaiming the good news of the kingdom and healing every disease and sickness. When he saw the crowds, he had compassion on them, because they were harassed and helpless, like sheep without a shepherd. Then he said to his disciples, "The harvest is plentiful but the workers are few. Ask the Lord of the harvest, therefore, to send out workers into his harvest field."
—Matthew 9:35–38

The very first sentence captures Jesus' actions—traveling, teaching, proclaiming the gospel (evangelizing), and healing. But did you notice the attitude motivating these actions? Jesus wasn't doing good things just to do them. He wasn't trying to please people or win a Christian character award. Jesus was driven by compassion. His *heart* was in it, not just His hands! If we want to catch the fire of God's mission, we have to start in the same place. We have to start with open hearts.

HOW DO MKS GET "ON MISSION"?

So what's step one? How do we cultivate a compassionate heart like Jesus? How do we step out of the hallway and engage in Christ's mission? I'm going to suggest five steps that will move you in the right direction.

START WITH PRAYER

The first step toward an open heart is asking God to open your eyes. Ask Him to help you see the people in your host country the way *He* sees them. Maybe you already have warm feelings toward the people in your host country. A lot of MKs I've encountered view their countries with pride and respect. But if resentment, disdain, or prejudice has crept into your perspective of the people and culture surrounding you, you must repent. Before God, acknowledge your ugly heart attitudes. Be honest! He can handle it, and He will love you through it. Admit that your ungodly attitudes are sins against the Creator who made all mankind in His image. Ask God to forgive you and to change your heart. Remember, grace does not just have the power to save us; it also has the power to transform us. You've been saved by grace, so *live* by grace (Colossians 2:6; Galatians 3:3). Rely on God's grace to give you a heart for the people He loves so much.

PURSUE LOVE

You've prayed and invited God to work in your heart. Now what? How does God want *you* specifically to participate in making disciples of all nations? It's a hard question! After all, there are so many wonderful ways to minister to lost people. You could start a Bible club for neighborhood kids. You could give gospel tracts and warm blankets to the poor. You could blog. You could volunteer at an orphanage. You could bust out a guitar and start a praise band in the park! *Where do you begin?*

Author and Bible teacher Beth Moore would say, "Begin with love." Pursue love for Christ, and watch as the rest becomes clear. In her study on 1 and 2 Thessalonians, *Children of the Day*, she writes: "When you are teeming with love for the Lord your God, who are you right then? What is your passion? What are you bursting to do when your heart is flooded with divine affection? That's very likely the stream of your calling. Take a step and get your feet wet."

Beloved child of God, there is no one else on this planet just like you. God has given you unique passions and gifts, and your love for Jesus is the spark that will ignite them! Beth Moore goes on to write, "You don't have to figure out what to surrender to. Just surrender every ounce of your heart to Jesus. Ask Him to give you a supernatural love for Him that surpasses anything in your human experience." Ministry flows out of that love. It can overflow into passionate teaching or writing, into acts of mercy toward the poor, into advocacy for the oppressed, into one-on-one evangelism, or into broad seed sowing. The possibilities are limitless.

MINISTER THROUGH YOUR REALMS OF INFLUENCE

As your heart and your passions come together, it's time to answer some practical questions. Colossians 4:5 instructs believers to "be wise in the way you act toward outsiders; make the most of *every opportunity*" (author's emphasis). In order to make the most of every opportunity to share our faith, we must first identify the opportunities God has set before us. Think about your daily life and ask yourself: When and where do I come in contact with lost people? At school? In my neighborhood or sports clubs? At the market? On vacation?

I used to think I had no opportunities to share my faith because I went to a Christian school, so I was never around lost people. But in reality, I just didn't notice all the opportunities right in front of me. Once a week I walked past a squatter village on my way to ballet class. I saw the same destitute families over and over again. I just never stopped to offer them anything, least of all the gospel. I saw lost people at the mall, at restaurants, and at every red light when they would beg for money at our car windows. But I wasn't thinking creatively about how to reach them for Christ.

What about you? When and where do you come in contact with lost people? Go ahead and get out a sheet of paper and make a list. God may even lay specific people on your heart as you brainstorm. Keep that list handy! The more missions-minded you become, the more God will open your eyes, and the more your list of opportunities will grow.

PARTNER WITH OTHERS

Perhaps by now a missional idea or two is already starting to simmer in the back of your brain. (If all you hear are crickets, don't worry! God is not in a hurry, remember? He'll get us there!) Let's turn our attention toward something the Bible talks about a lot—community. Making disciples of all nations was never meant to be an independent assignment. Who could join you in reaching the lost? Who could you *challenge* to partner with you? In eighth grade a friend named Crystal invited me to tag along with a group who was going to share their faith with strangers at the mall. I had never done anything like that before. I went, more out of curiosity than passion. But somewhere along the way, listening to the stories of strangers, I caught hold of the passion. I saw them the way Jesus saw them, "harassed and helpless , like sheep without a shepherd" (Matthew 9:36). Crystal casually issued an invitation that impacted eternity. She changed the strangers' lives, and she changed my life.

Who could you partner with in reaching the lost? A friend? A sibling? A younger student who looks up to you? Who could you enlist to pray with you? You've probably heard or even memorized Matthew 18:20, "For where two or three gather in my name, there am I with them." But the real question is, do you apply it? Do you rely on the body of Christ to experience the presence and power of Christ? Even great pioneers of evangelism, like the Apostle Paul, did not attempt to run the race alone. He partnered with Timothy, Silas, and others.

As you ask God to open your eyes to potential partners, don't forget those two older folks who think the world of you. Not only do your parents know your gifts and personality, they just may have a dozen ideas for how you could minister alongside them.

MEET PHYSICAL AND SPIRITUAL NEEDS

Finally, consider how you can meet both physical and spiritual needs. Jesus did this all the time. He healed a blind man, then offered him salvation (John 9:1–7, 35–38). He forgave a lame man's sins, then made him walk again (Matthew 9:1–8). In James 2:15–17, James uses an anecdote to explain the link between faith and good works. He writes: "Suppose a brother or a sister is without clothes and daily food. If one of you says to them, 'Go in peace; keep warm and well fed,' but does nothing about their physical needs, what good is it? In the same way, faith by itself, if it is not accompanied by action, is dead."

True believers put feet to their faith, becoming *doers* of the Word and not just *hearers* of the Word (James 1:22). Why? Because compassion cannot be contained. It bleeds into action. Often, taking practical action to meet someone's physical needs opens the door to meeting their spiritual needs. It demonstrates tangible love to them.

Shortly after going to the mall with Crystal, my eighth grade Bible class decided to do a Christmas service project. For months we collected clothes, toys, and canned goods. Then one day we wrapped them in Christmas paper, tucked in some gospel tracts, and loaded everything into a van. Our first stop was beneath a bridge my school bus passed every day. I had seen the people living under that bridge for years, but to my shame, they were just a landmark on the way to school.

Not that morning. That morning I stepped into their world. As I climbed off the van I choked on the hot, smoggy air. Cars whizzed by on either side as my classmates and I hauled our packages beneath the bridge. It smelled of exhaust fumes and waste, and before long my ears were ringing with the constant drum of speeding cars and blaring horns. As my eyes adjusted to the darkness, I began to see small children venturing out of the shadows. There were so many of them! Twenty? Thirty? They vastly outnumbered the adults, and some of them were so young they could barely walk. All of them were naked. I remember that very clearly because their skin was covered with open scabs.

Hesitantly, the children approached us, their eyes wide with curiosity. The adults were more interested in the packages we brought, but the children couldn't stop staring at these fair-skinned visitors. Impulsively, one of my classmates lifted a small toddler into her arms. The reaction was swift and startling! Children swarmed her, their skinny arms raised high. Even the ones who could barely walk eagerly reached for her.

I couldn't believe it. They didn't want our toys or clothes; they wanted to be held. They wanted our love! I wondered how often anyone ever held them. One by one, my entire class got on our knees, our arms outstretched. The kids flocked to us like cattle, herded into our hugs. They sat on our knees, hung on our shoulders, clung to our backs. I had never seen *need* like this before in my life. It was an ocean of heartache too deep for me to swim in.

I wouldn't have set foot under that bridge if not for my eighth grade teacher and her conviction to meet physical needs. *What are the physical needs of those around you?* Think about the people you pass every day. How could your family or friends work together to practically meet their needs and point them to Jesus?

Maybe you don't live in a culture where the physical needs are overwhelming. A missionary to a European country once told me how intimidating it is to minister to a people group that has so few physical needs. She and her husband were trying to share the gospel with people who were wealthier, more successful, and more educated than they were. "All we have to give them is the gospel," she said. "And yet, is there anything more valuable to offer?"

As my friend and her husband invested deeply in the lives of these people, they began to see how they could meet their emotional needs for friendship, empathy, wise counsel, and a listening ear. Instead of offering these wealthy people warm clothes and food, they offered them experiences that would interest them. They hosted American cooking classes and family festivals, things that intrigued their European friends and eventually built bridges to sharing the gospel.

How we engage in Christ's mission will look different for all of us. It depends on our personalities, passions, and cultural context. But there will be one common denominator: a heart like Christ's. Are you ready to offer God your whole heart and hang on for the ride? First John 5:14–15 says, "This is the confidence we have in approaching God: that if we ask anything according to his will, he hears us. And if we know that he hears us . . . we know that we have what we asked of him." If you ask God to open your eyes to His mission and to give you opportunities to fulfill it, He *will* grant your request. Beloved MK, the harvest is plentiful, but the workers are few. You're already on the harvest field. Won't you join the workers?

QUESTIONS FOR REFLECTION

What is the predominant religion or belief system in your host culture? Briefly explain or journal the major tenets of this religion or belief system.

Reread Beth Moore's quote: "When you are teeming with love for the Lord your God, who are you right then? What is your passion?" Finish this sentence:

When my heart is filled with love for Jesus, I am passionate about . . .

What are some of the greatest needs (physical or spiritual) among people in your host culture?

Look at the following list of ideas for missional living. Based on your personality, passions, and cultural context, circle any of the ideas that interest you*:

- volunteering in a homeless shelter, crisis pregnancy center, orphanage, etc.
- creating a sports club or Bible club for neighborhood kids
- blogging about Christian living, your country, important causes, etc.
- handing out food and supplies to the poor
- sharing your faith in a public place (such as a park, college campus, or the mall)
- starting a Bible study with peers
- teaching a local Sunday School class
- hosting a free cooking workshop with a short gospel presentation
- working with friends to create a Vacation Bible School in your setting
- writing a column in your parents' prayer letters

What ideas could you add to this list?

Who could you enlist to partner with you?

*Many of these ideas require adult supervision. Always make sure you have your parents' support and permission before attempting a missional project.

CHAPTER 10

A FRESH PERSPECTIVE ON FURLOUGH

My brother, sister, and I obediently shuffled into the potential supporters' home. We were on furlough, and already we had spent a few months in the US, my dad's home country. Now we were in Singapore, my mom's home country, and we knew the drill. The adults would chat, we would eat dinner, and then our parents would show these nice people a slideshow of their ministry. (I had every single slide memorized by the time I was in fifth grade. My dad didn't stray from his speech by a single syllable. Ever.) After, my parents would challenge the viewers to join our support team.

You would think something so routine was predictable. But there were always unexpected elements: sometimes the homes were gorgeous and ornate, sometimes they smelled like wet dogs. Sometimes the potential supporters had lots of young kids racing around, and sometimes they only had oxygen tanks for company. Nevertheless, no matter what we encountered, my siblings and I knew the five cardinal rules of support dinners:

1. Don't touch anything.
2. Answer adults politely when they talk to you.
3. Be nice to their children *no matter what*.
4. Fight with one another, and you will be grounded for life.

And of course, the biggie:

5. Eat whatever they put in front of you.

Everything went smoothly until dinnertime. We gathered around the fancy table, and our beaming Singaporean hostess brought out a giant bowl of steaming hair soup. I promise I'm not joking! It's actually called *hair soup*. Imagine cutting off someone's long, black hair and dropping it in water. That's exactly what hair soup looks like . . . and tastes like too. The black noodles are so thin and uniquely textured that it actually feels like hair is sliding down your throat. The moment the bowls were set on the table, my brother, sister, and I shot our mom desperate glances. My mom and dad exchanged looks. They knew this was asking a lot of us. At last my mom caught my eye and motioned slightly with her head. I understood exactly what she was giving me permission to do. The minute the hostess disappeared into the kitchen and her husband was distracted, I dumped my entire bowl of "hair" into my dad's bowl. *Plop!*

The next time they weren't looking, my brother dumped his. *Plop!* And then my sister. *Plop!* To this day, I don't know how my dad managed it, but there must've been a gallon of hairy noodles in his belly by the time we walked out the front door! I never did ask if that sweet couple actually joined our support team, but for my dad's sake I sure hope they did!

MISSIONAL LIVING WHILE ON FURLOUGH

Most mission organizations refer to a short trip back to your passport country as a furlough. It's an opportunity to rest, see extended family members, and raise financial support if necessary. In the last chapter we talked about becoming missional in our host countries. But what does missional living look like when we're on furlough in our parents' home countries?

We can probably all agree there are some major perks to furlough: being spoiled by Grandma and Grandpa, watching TV shows in your native tongue, stuffing your face with all those delicacies you've been missing for so long. But furlough can also be intimidating. When you haven't visited a place in years, there's bound to be culture shock. You may say the wrong thing, order the wrong food, or take 20 minutes to convert money in your head to see if that shirt is actually a good bargain. It's like swimming upstream—possible, but altogether exhausting. Not to mention, furlough usually involves significant traveling. Sleeping in other people's homes. Eating their (potentially hair-like) food. Being on your best behavior for months on end. It's safe to say, fishbowl syndrome is at fever pitch during furlough!

To top it off, longer furloughs may mean transitioning into a new school for a while. Can we all agree that teachers + culture shock + hundreds of teenagers = major anxiety?! It doesn't take more than ten minutes on a new campus to recognize all the ways you stand out. Wrong shoes, wrong jeans, wrong lingo. Then of course, there's the inevitable lapse in pop culture knowledge. And somewhere in between shopping for the right clothes and googling celebrities, you're also supposed to make new friends, find new classrooms, adjust to new teachers, pass tests, try out for sports teams, stomach the cafeteria food . . . oh yeah, and be on mission for Jesus. *Seriously?!*

In the wake of so much stress and insecurity, it's easy to forget the call to know Christ and make Him known. When you're choking on hair soup, it's easier to resent raising support than it is to be grateful for the chance to share in Christ's work. When you don't fit in at school, it's easier to look down on your seemingly culturally ignorant classmates than it is to take your pain to God and ask Him to help you see your peers the way He sees them. But costly obedience is at the very heart of the gospel! Jesus didn't obey the Father only when it was convenient, fun, or easy. He obeyed when it was agonizing. Only when it is truly difficult to obey can our faith be proven most faithful and our love most genuine.

BE HONEST

OK, so you've just stepped off the airplane and spotted your relatives waving like maniacs with tears in their eyes. You've got two months or six months or maybe a year or more for this furlough. You want to live a missional life, making the most of every opportunity to point others to Jesus. But where do you begin?

For starters, give yourself permission to be completely *honest* with God in the weeks and months to come. It may sound like a strange place to start, but honesty is crucial to emotional and spiritual health. We've already said there are going to be challenges and adjustments while on furlough. Those adjustments will evoke all sorts of feelings in your heart: excitement, frustration, anxiety, irritation. Talk to God about all of it! He is your perfect Father, and He can handle it. He already knows how you feel, but there's such freedom in *telling* Him. Use words, tears, or journal entries. Any way you want to do it, pour out your heart to Him—the good, the bad, and the ugly!

A woman named Hannah did this once. She was devastated that she could not have children and the Bible says, "In her *deep anguish* Hannah prayed to the LORD, *weeping bitterly*" (1 Samuel 1:10, author's emphasis). In fact, she prayed so fervently, a priest named Eli thought she was drunk! Listen to what Hannah told Eli: "'Not so, my lord,' Hannah replied, 'I am a woman who is *deeply troubled*. I have not been drinking wine or beer; I was *pouring out my soul to the LORD* . . . I have been praying here out of my great anguish and grief'" (vv. 15–16, author's emphasis).

Are you deeply troubled that your friends back in Argentina are making memories without you? Do you feel insecure every day at school? Are you exhausted by the traveling? Do you miss your own bed? Pour out your heart to the Lord.

CULTIVATE GRATITUDE

Just as it's important to be honest with God, it's also important not to get stuck in our negative feelings. Notice what Hannah does. After Eli confronts her, he tells her to "Go in peace," and the Bible says, "Then she went her way and ate something, and her face was no longer downcast" (vv. 17–18). Hannah was honest about her grief, but she chose not to wallow in it forever. She got up, ate something, and went on her way. Regardless of how she felt, she made the choice to stand up and keep going. This demonstrates faith in God. When we pour out our concerns to God but then worry about them all night long, complain about them constantly, and sulk endlessly, we prove that we don't trust God. First Peter 5:7 says, "Cast all your anxiety on him because he cares for you." What's the point of casting our cares on Jesus if we pick them right back up again?

Let's leave those burdens at Jesus' feet and begin to cultivate gratitude instead of anxiety. In her book *Choosing Gratitude*, Nancy Leigh DeMoss writes, "Gratitude has a big job to do in us and in our hearts. And it is one of the chief ways that God infuses joy and resilience into the daily struggle of life." Joy and gratitude are kind of like best friends. Any time one shows up, you'll find the other close by. That means the more you cultivate gratitude, the more you'll be surprised by joy, even in the midst of hardship.

Gratitude is both a result of God's grace and a choice we make. DeMoss goes on to write, "Gratitude is a lifestyle. A hard-fought, grace-infused, biblical lifestyle." How can we work to develop gratitude? Here are a few ideas:

- Keep a gratitude journal.
- Make a list of three new things for which you are thankful every day.
- Use a concordance to look up Bible verses about gratitude, and memorize your favorites.
- Rather than complaining, use a grateful tone when posting on social media.
- When you catch yourself about to complain (out loud or in your mind), stop and talk about one thing you're thankful for.
- Make a list of everything you like and dislike about furlough. Thank God for the things you like. Beside each item you dislike, write down one reason you can give thanks. (For instance, you may dislike your new school, but you can thank God that He is always with you, even at school.)

These are just suggestions. The best ideas are ones God lays on your heart! So invite Him into your journey. Be honest about all your yuckiest feelings . . . but don't get stuck there. God has so much better for you!

ASK GOD FOR COMPASSION AND CONVICTION

Finally, just as you ask God to give you compassion and conviction in your host country, ask Him for compassion and conviction while on furlough. Ask Him to open your eyes to the lost people around you. Invite Him to speak through you. Several times, God has burdened me to share the gospel with another person. Sometimes it's someone I know, and sometimes it's a total stranger. But when I feel that prompting, I immediately start praying, "OK, God, please give me courage! Speak through me. I don't know what to say, but You do!"

When it comes to missional living, much of the battle lies in simply being *willing* to be used by God. We must pray for hearts like the prophet Isaiah, who saw God's glory, heard God's call, and cried, "Here am I. Send me!" (See Isaiah 6:1–8.)

ON MISSION AMONG FELLOW MKS

We've discussed being missional in our host countries and on furlough in our passport countries. But there is one other people group within your realm of influence who desperately needs the gospel, and that's fellow MKs. Sadly, it's taken me decades to realize this. Growing up, I never viewed my MK peers as people in need of the gospel. I assumed they needed the gospel like an Eskimo needs snow. After all, they had Christian parents, church, Bible class, mission conferences . . . they were virtually drowning in Christianity!

But I was so deceived. The gospel isn't like that old ham sandwich everyone is sick of. The gospel is like *air!* We need it to live and breathe. Without it, we are hopeless. The problem is, we have such a narrow perspective of what sharing the gospel means. We hear those words and imagine reciting our testimony or pulling out a pamphlet. But just as Paul learned to "become all things to all people," we must learn how to share the gospel differently depending on our audience (1 Corinthians 9:19–23). In Christian circles, we call this "contextualization."

For instance, a nine-year-old African girl you meet on a mission trip probably needs you to pull out a pamphlet with pictures that will help you explain the gospel. A 15-year-old atheist you're befriending on furlough would greatly benefit from hearing your testimony. But your MK pal who just found out she's moving again probably doesn't need either of those things. *But that doesn't mean she doesn't need the gospel.* She just needs it to be shared contextually. She needs to be reminded that God has a plan for her life. She needs the comfort of knowing He will never leave her. And she needs the conviction of realizing that Jesus has sacrificed far more for her than He will ever ask her to sacrifice for Him. In other words, you have the opportunity to help her see how the gospel relates to her specific circumstances. Even if she's already a believer, she needs this hope to refresh and sustain her. And don't forget, there's always the chance she's not yet a true believer.

As I write these words, the faces of my grown MK friends who have turned their backs on God fill my mind. Oh, how I wish I had not assumed every MK was a true believer! How I wish the gospel had so filled my life that it bubbled over in every setting—among the lost, among the saved, on furlough, at home, and with MKs.

QUESTIONS FOR REFLECTION

What are some of the things you love the most about furlough?

What are some of the things you dislike the most?

Have you ever thought about sharing your faith when you're on furlough? If so, when do you consider doing it? (Example: Around family members? At school? With neighbors?)

Reread the list of ideas for cultivating gratitude. Which of these suggestions would you like to consider putting into practice? Are there any other ideas you could add to this list?

Do you know any MKs who are going through a difficult time? How could you help them see their trials in light of the gospel?

CHAPTER 11

WHAT I CAN (AND CAN'T) PROMISE YOU

As I sit here writing this book, it's almost Christmastime. This morning we decorated our tree, and before long the whole house was filled with the smell of pine needles and hot chocolate, the twinkle of lights and glitter, and the jingle of Christmas carols. That's what I love about Christmas—it completely takes over a house, flooding our senses with joy and anticipation.

In my final chapter to you, dear MKs, I want to leave you with the same sense of all-consuming joy and anticipation. Only in this case, it's rooted in something far greater than pine needles and hot chocolate! I want to point you to the reward God has in store for all true believers. I alluded to this reward several times throughout the book as we examined suffering. But now I want to dig deeply into it—to light it on fire like a Christmas candle and let its lovely aroma invade our hearts. Let me begin by taking you back in time several years to Moby Arena, a stadium at Colorado State University.

THE FLAG PARADE

Every other year, Cru missionaries from around the world assembled at Colorado State University for a staff conference. One night we gathered in the stadium for an evening ceremony. I don't remember the order of events; all I remember is what happened at the end. A man came on stage and began announcing different countries. Each time he named a country, a group of people bearing a flag for that country paraded across the stage, and part of the audience clapped. "What are they doing?" I whispered to my mom.

"Those are our new staff," my mom whispered back. "They've agreed to serve God in that country. The people clapping are the missionaries that already serve in that country."

"Oh." I began to make out little clusters of people cheering at different times throughout the stadium. "Yay, Brazil!" "Woohoo, Sweden!" "Go, Colombia!" It was like a pep rally, where everyone cheers for their own team. At last the flag I was waiting for made its way across the stage, and I clapped along with the rest of my family. "Hooray, Philippines!" I checked out the array of families who would be joining our efforts in the country I loved.

Finally the curtains parted, and one last flag came out. Unlike the others, only two small Asian women carried this flag. Suddenly, the entire auditorium erupted in thunderous applause. People whistled and jumped to their feet. The bleachers vibrated. It was so sudden I nearly leapt out of my skin. "What's going on?" I yelled to my mom. "Why is everyone clapping?"

With tears in her eyes, my mom looked down and said, "That's the flag for China!"

When the ceremony was over, she finally explained it to me. China is a closed country where Christians face extreme persecution. Those two women had come to faith in Christ while in America, and they were pledging to return to China as native missionaries. As Chinese nationals, they had a great advantage for spreading the gospel in this hostile environment. However, they also faced much graver risks.

I thought about those women for a long time after the parade. As an MK, the vast majority of my suffering was not of my own choosing. It was the result of decisions beyond my control. But that wasn't the case for these women. They were *choosing* this very difficult lifestyle for themselves.

Why? Why would anyone choose a path that led straight through the fire? Unless . . . those two women understood something I did not.

SHIPWRECKS, STONES, AND OPEN SEA

Ambrose Redmoon once wrote, "Courage is not the absence of fear, but rather the judgment that something else is more important than one's fear." In other words, when a firefighter runs into a burning building, it's not because he or she is fearless. The firefighter realizes the flames are hot, the smoke is real, and the structure could collapse, but he or she believes the *people* trapped in the building are *more important* than fear. And that's what gives him or her courage.

When it comes to the cause of Christ, you and I will only be willing to endure suffering and danger to the extent that we *value* Christ's mission and His promised reward. In his lifetime, the Apostle Paul experienced more danger and suffering than you and I could likely fathom. Listen to this list:

> Five times I received from the Jews the forty lashes minus one. [*That's approximately 195 lashes, in case you're wondering!*] Three times I was beaten with rods, once I was pelted with stones, three times I was shipwrecked, I spent a night and a day in the open sea, I have been constantly on the move. I have been in danger from rivers, in danger from bandits, in danger from my fellow Jews, in danger from Gentiles; in danger in the city, in danger in the country, in danger at sea; and in danger from false believers. I have labored and toiled and have often gone without sleep; I have known hunger and thirst and have often gone without food; I have been cold and naked. Besides everything else, I face daily the pressure of my concern for all the churches. —2 Corinthians 11:24–28

And we thought *we* had it bad! Maybe you feel like you can relate to being constantly on the move or maybe even some of the dangers . . . but a night and day *in open sea*? Beaten with rods? *Stoned?* Scholars who have studied the life of Paul believe he was likely deformed due to the extent of the beatings he endured. Taking all of this into account, do you think Paul was ever scared? Do you think he ever felt discouraged? I know he did. In fact, he admits it. In 2 Corinthians 1:8, he says he and Timothy endured such hardship in Asia that they despaired of life itself.

So the big question is, why didn't he just quit? He was an accomplished, gifted man who could have done many things with his life. Why would he continue to put himself in dangerous, painful situations? Paul answers this very question in Philippians 3:7–9:

> But whatever were gains to me I now consider loss for the sake of Christ. What is more, I consider everything a loss because of the surpassing worth of knowing Christ Jesus my Lord, for whose sake I have lost all things. I consider them garbage, that I may gain Christ and be found in him, not having a righteousness of my own that comes from the law, but that which is through faith in Christ—the righteousness that comes from God on the basis of faith.

Paul knew the dangers and suffering that accompanied his calling. But he also knew the reward. Did you catch what the reward is? Paul says everything in his life is like garbage compared to the surpassing worth of *knowing Christ and being found righteous in Christ*. In other words, the reward is the gospel! It's Christ Himself. It's the chance to *know* Him . . . not know *about* Him, the way you know about George Washington. It's a chance to actually *know* Him, the way you know your best friend. It's the chance to let His righteousness cover all your wickedness so that you're free to live by grace. It's the chance to rest in His goodness and be saved by His grace.

Just for a moment, think of all the good things in your life—friends, family, your phone—think of everything you love the most! Paul's not saying that your best friend, baby brother, or smartphone is garbage. He's saying that Jesus Christ is *so great* everything else seems like garbage *in comparison*! Nothing can compete with Him. Not popularity, stuff, accomplishments, or relationships—none of it can hold a candle to Jesus. Jesus is the reward your heart is longing for.

When I left the Philippines as a 15-year-old, I knew this fact in my head, but I didn't believe it in my heart. I believed that the boy I liked and the friends I idolized were a better reward than Jesus. I valued them more than Jesus.

Precious MK, it's time to ask yourself a hard question: what do you value most? If you value comfort more than anything else, you will hate God every time He asks you to give it up. If you value friendships more than anything else, you will despise your parents every time they make you move. But if you value Jesus more than anything else, He will empower you to sacrifice everything for His glory. And in exchange, He will give you everything your heart truly desires. He will give you the greatest reward: a deepening personal relationship with Christ Himself.

Guess what? You can take that reward to every single country on the face of the planet. Nobody can ever steal it from you. It can't die, get lost in customs, or make new friends and abandon you. The reward of Jesus Christ is permanent. It means you always have a home. You always have a friend. You always have purpose. You always have value. You always have hope, and it stretches way past 7th grade and college and marriage and old age . . . all the way into eternity. You have hope *forever.*

WHEN YOU'VE WANDERED FAR AWAY

As we approach the end of this book, maybe you're thinking, *But what if I'm just not there? What if I don't value Jesus most? What if I don't value Him at all? What if I've wandered so far away I'm completely lost?*

Jesus tells a story about a scenario like this. He paints the picture of a shepherd with 100 sheep. One of them wanders away. Let's just say he's the sheep who's so unruly Dad and Mom have been asked to leave the mission field. Or maybe he's the sheep living a double life, pretending to know all the answers when secretly he's so caught in sin that he doesn't even believe the Shepherd is real. In any case, he's utterly lost. As every good shepherd knows, this means the sheep is in grave danger. Listen to what Jesus says:

> If a man owns a hundred sheep, and one of them wanders away, will he not leave the ninety-nine on the hills and go to look for the one that wandered off? And if he finds it, truly I tell you, he is happier about that one sheep than about the ninety-nine that did not wander off. —Matthew 18:12–13

Dear lost sheep, the truth is you can't find the way back. Not by yourself. You need to turn from your sin and cry out to the Shepherd. He alone can rescue you. *Repentance* is the biblical term for turning away from sin and turning toward Jesus. Acts 3:19 says, "Repent, then, and *turn to God*, so that your sins may be wiped out" (author's emphasis). Repentance is an act of the heart. No one can fake it or force it. It is prompted by the Holy Spirit at work in you.

If you long to turn from your sin and cry out to Jesus, do it today! Do it right this minute. You don't have to use big words or say anything fancy. You just have to mean it.

A few days ago my daughter confessed to committing a sin I knew nothing about. She climbed into my lap with tears streaming down her cheeks. "Mommy," she whispered, "I want to tell you something . . ." And with her small, kindergarten vocabulary, she told me. She came clean. There was nothing grand about the apology, but she *meant* it.

That's what you need to do. If you've wandered far from God, you need to climb into His lap, and just tell Him. Admit that you're guilty, and ask Him to forgive you. Throw yourself upon His mercy. *He's already chasing you*. And He alone can carry you back.

If you do these things—if you turn to God, if you surrender to His plan instead of yours—I cannot promise you an easy life. I can't promise that your parents will raise all their support, enjoy fruitful ministry, or always understand you. I can't promise that saying goodbye will ever get easier or that your friends won't move on without you. I can't promise you won't spend some nights crying into your pillow or wishing God would write the story of your life differently.

But this is what I *can* promise you: I promise God sees you—struggling to fit in, scared of being exposed, hiding in the hallway. I promise that if you step out of that hallway and embrace the call to know Him and make Him known, your life will not be wasted. I promise He will walk with you. I promise He will never abandon you. I promise the eternal reward of following Christ will outshine all the suffering you ever endure on earth. And I promise that when it's finally time to run into His arms, you won't regret a single sacrifice you made for Him.

QUESTIONS FOR REFLECTION

Read Philippians 3:7–11. Why was Paul willing to endure so much suffering for the sake of Jesus?

What is the ultimate reward for following Christ?

Paul wrote that he willingly lost all things for the sake of Christ. What are some things you are not willing to give up for the sake of Christ? In other words, what are some things you value more than Jesus? Take a moment and confess these idols to God. Ask Him to help you love Him more than anything else.

Could you relate to the parable of the lost sheep? If so, how? If you made the decision to repent and turn to Christ, tell your parents about it.

What are two or three of the biggest things God taught you through reading this book?

Are there any changes you need to make in your life? If so, what are they? Discuss these thoughts with your parents.

CHAPTER 12

A NOTE TO PARENTS

In 1985 my mother traveled 7,000 miles across the globe with an infant and a three-year-old daughter. *7,000 miles.* (And I thought taking four children to the grocery store was a feat!) I was the infant. My mom and dad were finishing up furlough in the US, and my Singaporean mother did not have American citizenship yet. She needed a few more weeks to finish the process of being naturalized. But ministry in the Philippines could not wait, so my dad went on ahead of her.

After officially being sworn in as a US citizen, my mom began planning for the long journey back to the Philippines. She thought of everything— toys, snacks, diapers, pacifiers, and, most importantly, Benadryl, which several friends assured her would send the crankiest kid straight to sleep on an airplane. Next came the cargo. She packed suitcases to check and carry-on bags she could sling over one shoulder. She packed a stroller for me and a small backpack my three-year-old sister could carry independently. "Johanna," my mom prepped my sister, "when we go on this trip, I need you to be Mommy's big helper. Can you do that?" My sister nodded solemnly. For days Johanna practiced toddling around the house with her backpack snug on her shoulders. We were all set!

On the morning of our journey, we woke before dawn and set off. Amazingly, in the hours it took to drive to the airport, get through security, check our suitcases, and fly to New York, my sister didn't take a single nap. When at last we settled in our seats for the 15-hour flight to Seoul, my mom gave her wide-eyed toddler a dose of Benadryl, positive she would finally fall asleep. But Johanna had never taken Benadryl before, and unfortunately (as it does for some children) it had the opposite effect. My poor mother may as well have injected her with a quart of caffeine. Little Johanna went buck wild, bouncing around her seat like a maniac. For 15 hours, my mom tried desperately to subdue her hyperactive toddler and fussy baby.

At last the plane landed, and my mom hurriedly collected our carry-on bags. She had a small window of time to go from one end of the airport to the other to catch a connecting flight. "Johanna!" She barked at my sister. "Time to be Mommy's big helper! Hold your backpack." Glancing up, she saw my sister sprawled across the airplane seat, snoring loudly. My mother shook her. "Wake up! It's time to go!" Nothing. She was in a drug-induced, sleep-deprived coma.

I'll never know how she did it, but somehow my tiny mother managed to shove me into the stroller, heave all our bags into her arms, throw my sleeping sister on top, and elbow her way off the plane, across the airport, and onto her connecting flight!

A MILE IN YOUR SHOES

The first time I heard the story of my mom's ill-fated flight across the Pacific Ocean, I laughed uproariously. I was probably 11 or 12. (It's quite likely she repressed the memory for the first decade of my life.) Now, as a mom of four small children, I cringe with pity. What a nightmare! OK . . . I still laugh a little . . . but *what a nightmare!*

Truth be told, this has been a challenging chapter to write for one simple reason: I have never walked a mile in your shoes. In all my experiences overseas, I was never the mom racing through the airport with babies and baggage in tow. I was the baby snoozing in the stroller . . . or the kid along for the adventure . . . or the teen struggling to fit in. But I was not the parent making major family decisions or lying awake at night wondering if I did the right thing or praying fervently for the futures of my children. I didn't bear the responsibility of being in charge or of shielding my little ones from burdens and fears they couldn't imagine.

For that reason, I write this chapter with great humility. If I were a missionary with grown children and a wealth of parental wisdom, I would offer it to you. But I am not. What I *can* offer, however, is a small voice for your child.

Recently, I had the opportunity to hear John Piper's son, Barnabas, speak at a conference. He used a simple but powerful analogy to describe the experience of being raised as a ministry kid. He said that when he was young, he went to a private school where rocks lined the sidewalk. Barnabas liked collecting rocks, so every day he picked up one or two rocks to add to his collection. One day a school administrator noticed what he was doing and stopped him. Barnabas protested that he was only taking one or two rocks, and there were plenty lining the sidewalk. But the administrator said, "There's over a hundred kids at this school. If everyone took a couple of rocks, there would be nothing left but dirt."

This captures the experience of a ministry kid, Barnabas explained. Everyone makes one or two small comments about how the ministry kid behaves, dresses, carries himself, or interacts with others. They have one or two expectations for the ministry kid, one or two standards they place upon the ministry kid. But what they don't realize is that all of these small comments, expectations, and standards add up to enormous pressure. Because everyone is taking a rock from the sidewalk.

Ministry kids, like preacher's kids and missionary kids, feel this pressure. I certainly did. It was the pressure to be good enough, the pressure that comes from being on display at churches, conferences, and supporters' homes. There was external pressure to live up to everyone's expectations for a missionary kid and internal pressure to find my identity as an individual when I was constantly viewed as an extension of my parents and their calling.

These mixed-up feelings were often intensified in seasons of transition and change. But I rarely had the maturity to understand my own emotions, let alone express them to my parents. As an adult I have more clarity. In some healing conversations with my own mom and dad, I've had the opportunity to finally express what I wanted and needed from them at key moments in my MK journey.

I would like to share some of those insights with you, in hope that God may use them to bless your own relationships with the precious MKs sleeping under your roof. I realize all children are unique, but I also believe there are some similar emotions most MKs face. So for just a moment, would you graciously allow me to be a voice for them in sharing five pleas?

Dear Dad and Mom,

Please listen to me.

Listen to me when it's convenient, and listen to me when it's not. Listen when I want to talk about something big and something small. This is one of the most powerful ways you can show me that I matter to you. When you lay everything else down and listen to me, it assures me that *I don't have to compete with your ministry.* I need to understand that Jesus loves and values me, and if you consistently set me aside so you can focus on ministry, it makes me feel threatened by Jesus and His calling. I feel as if He and I are on opposite teams, vying for your attention. Teach me that Jesus is supremely important. But with your time and choices, also teach me that Jesus says *I* am vastly important to Him and to you.

Sometimes when you are listening to me, you might realize *I* don't even understand what I'm trying to say! In these times, I need you to do more than just listen; I need you to draw me out. Ask me questions. Help me process what I'm thinking and feeling, and *always point me to the hope that is in Christ.* This can take a lot of time. But it will shape how I think, what I believe, and who I become.

Please empathize with me.

When I am upset about a reality of MK life, I need you to do more than explain why we have to do what we have to do. I need you to grieve with me. I need to know you realize what these decisions cost me. Despite what I say (or scream!) I don't necessarily need you to change your decision. God has ordained you with authority, not me. But I do need empathy. I need to know that my voice is heard, my opinion considered, and my heartache felt. Contrary to what you may think, acknowledging my feelings of disappointment will not intensify them. It will allow me to finally let them go. Before *I* can get over it, I need to believe that *you* get it. So talk with me, cry with me, and find ways to make the changes easier on me. Buy me clothes that help me fit in. Believe me when I tell you that nobody sits by me in youth group. You don't always have to be positive, and you can't always fix it. Sometimes, you just have to abide with me through the storm. It will be painful but, Dad and Mom, God will use it to grow my faith.

Please use discretion in what you share with me.

Be careful how you talk about ministry, co-workers, and leaders around me. If you are growing jaded toward ministry, without even realizing it, you're probably passing on a jaded perspective to me. I am not your friend or your spouse. I don't have the maturity to process your negative emotions in light of the gospel. When I think you are unhappy in ministry, I feel anxious and insecure.

This doesn't mean you have to be perfect. But when you blow it and vent or complain in front of me, don't leave things that way. Later, when God has refreshed you in His Word, come back and refresh me too. Teach me how to have a gospel-centered view of the difficulties our family faces. Explain to me again (and again) why it's worth it. Tell me again (and again) that God is faithful. Model perseverance not just outwardly with hands that do God's work but inwardly with a heart that trusts Him regardless of our circumstances. As I watch you trust God, I will learn to trust Him too.

Please connect me with godly community.

One of the best and worst things about being an MK is that few people share my experiences. While this makes me feel unique and special, it can also be very lonely and isolating. As a result, I long for community. I long for a sense of belonging, acceptance, and friendship. Helping me find godly community is one of the most relevant ways you can minister to me.

Depending on my personality, I may jump at the opportunity to meet new people, or I may resist it. But you know me! Help me work within my comfort zone to develop godly friendships at church, school, and within our ministry team. If there is an opportunity for me to attend a retreat or conference with other MKs, encourage me to participate. There will not be many chances for me to meet peers who share my experiences and emotions, and the connections I make with them will impact me powerfully.

Please be willing to take radical measures for me.

Finally, please be my greatest champion, cheerleader, and advocate. Unlike the people around you, I didn't arrive on your doorstep with marriage problems, addictions, or demonic bondage. I don't need the Bible translated into my language, clean water for my village, or lessons in basic sanitation for the sake of my survival. But that doesn't mean I don't need you just as much—and even more—than all the people around you.

Dad and Mom, please don't ever forget that I am the first ministry God has called you to. Many people can be missionaries, but only you can be my parents. I need you to take the time to deeply instill God's truth in me, to regularly pray over me, to counsel, lead, and shepherd me. And if push comes to shove and I'm drowning, I need you to take radical measures to rescue me.

Even if it means family counseling or relocation. Even if it means a demotion, homeschooling, or sabbatical. Even if it means leaving the mission field altogether. *Please do it!* If you have a sense in your spirit that I am really struggling, don't ignore it. Don't dismiss it as a phase or hope it will pass. Instead, commit to doing whatever God leads you to do for my sake. Commit to sacrificing anything and everything He asks you to sacrifice. Ultimately, you will be doing it for His sake as well as mine.

In case I rarely say it, thank you. Thank you for obeying Jesus, being my role models, and seeking to better understand me. One day I will realize just how much you have poured out your lives for me, how greatly you have served me, and how deeply you have loved me.

Always,
Your Child

TWO FINAL PROMISES

As I admitted earlier, all MKs are different and these five pleas are just a starting point. At the end of each chapter in this book, there are questions for reflection. In order to better understand your own MKs, you might consider discussing some of these questions with them. Peek into their brains; peer into their hearts. Maybe some of their thoughts and feelings will line up with mine, and likely many will be entirely original. Either way, not a moment will be wasted.

I cannot thank you enough for allowing your MK to take this journey with me. Before saying goodbye, I want to leave you with two promises. I already admitted I've never been a missionary. But I am a parent. I juggle marriage and children and ministry every single day. I wrestle with idolatry, anxiety, anger, and the all-elusive balancing act. I find it difficult to think of any calling on the planet more challenging than that of parenthood. And just when our little ones are becoming independent and we think the hardest part is over, we realize the work done with our hands is peanuts compared to the work done with our hearts. It is the most contradictory journey on earth—agonizing and jubilant, exhausting and rewarding, terrifying and comforting.

An older missionary once shared two principles with me as she reflected on her years parenting MKs: the certainty of hardship and the certainty of hope. These are the promises I want to leave with you. They may sound conflicting at first, but they actually go hand-in-hand, and together they provide anchors for our souls as parents.

THE CERTAINTY OF HARDSHIP

The first promise is that hard times will come. It's simply a guarantee. In this world, your children and mine will face difficulty, and when they do our hearts will ache inexpressibly. But if we can peek beneath the discouraging surface of this promise, we'll spot a glimmer of freedom. Peter once wrote, "Dear friends, do not be surprised at the fiery ordeal that has come on you to test you, as though something strange were happening to you" (1 Peter 4:12).

Do you see the glimmer of encouragement? When our children endure heartbreak, grapple with their faith, fall into sin, or trample our dreams, we can whisper to our souls, "Nothing strange is happening!" Is it painful? *Absolutely.* Devastating? *Yes.* But strange? *No.* Trials are to be expected. They are part of the Christian life. They are not signs that God has abandoned us.

I remember once hearing an aerobics instructor yell, "Get comfortable being uncomfortable!" At the time my legs were quivering like jelly, and I kind of wanted to slap her. But she was on TV, and I was in the living room. So I gritted my teeth and took it. She said it over and over: "Get comfortable being uncomfortable!" Later, as I nursed my sore muscles on the couch, I thought about that statement. Spiritually, I was walking through a very dark season in my life, and I could see no end to the trial stretching before me. I wondered, *What if I could train my heart the way this aerobics instructor was trying to train my muscles?* What if I could get comfortable with the idea that life was not meant to be comfortable? What if I could get comfortable with having to trust God uncomfortably? What if I could get comfortable with waiting uncomfortably? With being tested uncomfortably?

It stands to reason that if hardship is a certainty, then spiritual stamina is a necessity. But how do we train our hearts to endure, specifically when the trials involve our most precious treasures—our children? For starters, we need an army. We need authentic, Christlike community. Christians were never meant to journey alone, and yet many people in ministry suffer in silence. Perhaps we're scared to let others in or to admit our failures. Perhaps our ability to trust has been injured. Perhaps we're in a remote location with few believers nearby.

Yet God commands us to live in fellowship with other Christians, and with confidence Paul penned the words, "And my God will meet all your needs according to the riches of his glory in Christ Jesus" (Philippians 4:19). Is community an unmet need in your life? Ask your faithful Father to supply it. Ask Him to bring people into your life and to open your eyes to the people already there. Then step out in obedience and start building genuine, Christ-centered relationships. If it's unwise to confide in fellow church members because your husband is a church leader, reach out to pastor's wives from different congregations. Join a Bible study even if you have to drive a far distance. Meet that accountability partner for coffee and spill the beans (no pun intended!). In order to support your children, you need others supporting you.

Besides being in community, it is crucial to nourish ourselves in the Word. We all know this. It's Discipleship 101, probably among the first five things we teach a new believer. But have you ever considered the fact that nourishing *yourself* is one of the most profound ways you can nourish your *children*?

In his book, *Crazy Busy*, Kevin DeYoung cites a survey conducted by Ellen Galinsky in which more than a thousand school-aged children were asked what one thing they would change about how their parents' work affected them. Parents were surprised to discover that the children seldom wished for more time with them. Rather, the vast majority wished their parents were less tired and stressed. DeYoung borrows the term "secondhand stress" to describe the way children feel in a constantly frazzled environment.

As believers, where do we go to lay down our anxiety and refresh our souls? To de-frazzle our hearts? We go to the Word! As the deer pants for water, so our souls thirst for the living God (Psalm 42:1–2), who alone promises:

> Come to me, all you who are weary and burdened, and I will give you rest. Take my yoke upon you and learn from me, for I am gentle and humble in heart, and you will find rest for your souls. For my yoke is easy and my burden is light. —Matthew 11:28–30

We don't have to stumble through life bearing the anxiety and exhaustion of support-raising, fruitless ministries, or wayward children . . . not when we belong to a Father who urges us to cast *all* our anxiety on him because He cares for us (1 Peter 5:7).

Hard times in parenting are not a possibility; they are a certainty. But the God of the Bible offers us a trade: our exhaustion for His rest, our anxiety for His peace. As we take Him up on His offer, we anchor our families in the only foundation strong enough to survive the storms.

THE CERTAINTY OF HOPE

This brings us to the second promise: there is no set of MK struggles too great for God. I once heard a speaker say, "God is in a grace-matching program." Alongside every hardship He allows us to face, He offers us the grace to survive. The psalmist wrote:

Where can I go from your Spirit? Where can I flee from your presence? If I go up to the heavens, you are there; if I make my bed in the depths, you are there. If I rise on the wings of the dawn, if I settle on the far side of the sea, even there your hand will guide me, your right hand will hold me fast. If I say, "Surely the darkness will hide me and the light become night around me," even the darkness will not be dark to you; the night will shine like the day, for darkness is as light to you. —Psalm 139:7–12

Where can our children go from God's Spirit? Where can they flee from His presence? If they walk with Him, He is there. If they stray from Him, He is there. If they run to the farthest corners of sin or hide for decades in darkness, even the darkness will not be dark to God. There is nowhere on earth where His sovereign hand does not hold them fast. And even if a chapter in their story plunges us into the darkness, even there God's hand will guide us; His right hand will hold us fast.

One of my favorite hymns contains a stanza that recently leapt off the page to me. If you know the tune to *How Firm a Foundation*, you can sing this stanza aloud:

In every condition—in sickness, in health,
In poverty's vale, or abounding in wealth,
At home and abroad, on the land, on the sea,
As thy days may demand, shall thy strength ever be.

I love the final line, "As thy days may demand, shall thy strength ever be." Isn't it a beautiful promise? Each of our stories is different. Our days demand varying types and degrees of strength, and our gracious Father promises to supply all our needs. He promises to meet us where we are and walk us through the fire. He is in a grace-matching program. Dear believer—you whose beautiful feet are taking the gospel throughout the nations—as your days may demand, shall your strength ever be.

OTHER BOOKS FOR
TEENS
from NEW HOPE

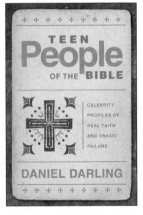

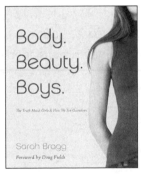

ISBN: 978-1-59669-444-6
N154122
$14.99

ISBN: 978-1-59669-319-7
N126101
$14.99

ISBN: 978-1-62591-504-7
N174103
$14.99

New Hope® Publishers is a division of WMU®, an international organization that challenges Christian believers to understand and be radically involved in God's mission. For more information about WMU, go to wmu.com. More information about New Hope books may be found at NewHopePublishers.com. New Hope books may be purchased at your local bookstore.

Please go to NewHopePublishers.com for more helpful information about *Hiding in the Hallway*.

If you've been blessed by this book, we would like to hear your story. The publisher and author welcome your comments and suggestions at: newhopereader@wmu.org.

NEW HOPE®
P U B L I S H E R S
Gospel-Centered. Missions-Driven.